The Paradox
of the Good Bribe

A person who avoids corruption is "somebody that just loves beefsteak but just can't bear to go to a slaughter pen because there are some bad, rough men down there who aren't animal lovers".

—Robert Penn Warren, *All the King's Men*, 1946

The Paradox
of the Good Bribe

A Discussion Defining
and Protecting
the Public Interest

David J O'Regan

Universal Publishers
Irvine • Boca Raton

The Paradox of the Good Bribe:
A Discussion Defining and Protecting the Public Interest

Universal Publishers, Inc.
Irvine • Boca Raton
USA • 2020
www.Universal-Publishers.com

978-1-62734-300-8 (pbk.)
978-1-62734-301-5 (ebk.)

Typeset by Medlar Publishing Solutions Pvt Ltd, India
Cover design by Ivan Popov

Library of Congress Cataloging-in-Publication Data

Names: O'Regan, David J, 1966- author.
Title: The paradox of the 'good' bribe : a discussion defining and
    protecting the public interest / David J O'Regan.
Description: Irvine : Universal Publishers, 2020. | Includes bibliographical
    references.
Identifiers: LCCN 2020004035 (print) | LCCN 2020004036 (ebook) |
    ISBN 9781627343008 (pbk.) | ISBN 9781627343015 (ebk.)
Subjects: LCSH: Bribery--Moral and ethical aspects. | Corruption--Moral
    and ethical aspects. | Public good--Moral and ethical aspects.
Classification: LCC HV6306 .O74 2020 (print) | LCC HV6306 (ebook) |
    DDC 179/.8--dc23
LC record available at https://lccn.loc.gov/2020004035
LC ebook record available at https://lccn.loc.gov/2020004036

I dedicate this book to Soumyadeep Bhattacharyya, whose clarity in perceiving ethical truth amid complexity and conflicting responsibilities has inspired me.

Table of Contents

Preface

This book contains reactions to a seemingly absurd suggestion. Four participants explore the ethical ramifications of a counterintuitive proposal that bribery might, on occasion, be harmless, or even virtuous.

The concept of virtuous bribery may seem, *prima facie*, preposterous. However, in our discussions, an economist puts forward strong arguments for the existence of the "good" bribe, which has a virtuous outcome, the "harmless" bribe, a *baksheesh* payment that simply encourages someone to speed up the performance of their existing duties without additional favors, and the "ambiguous" bribe, which arises from the frequent difficulty of differentiating an influence-peddling bribe from a gift given with no expectation of a *quid pro quo*. Our economist bases his arguments on the intentions behind and the consequences of the transactions, within a framework of radically *laissez-faire* markets. (He also seems, sometimes, to argue on the more straightforward grounds of economic expediency.)

A classicist and a Roman Catholic priest challenge the economist's views, using arguments that bribery is inherently undesirable, irrespective of its consequences. Their viewpoints are founded on traditional ethical lines, derived from the classical Greek virtues and biblical divine commands. The fourth participant, a student of French literature, introduces perspectives derived from critical social theory.

She draws attention to the ways in which bribery might tend to reinforce undesirable or illegitimate power structures, and she challenges the opinions offered not only by the economist but also by his two culturally conservative opponents. She shares with the economist a rather radical temperament, but her radicalism is founded on quite different assumptions.

The discussion reveals the strengths, weaknesses, and ambiguities of the different viewpoints and not infrequently exposes the limitations of dogmatic assertions. In a dramatization along the lines of a Platonic dialogue, the discussion's structure blends form and content to permit the interplay of a plurality of views, without necessarily providing a sole, definitive answer. Although the exchanges of ideas move in the direction of a tentative attempt at a reconciliation of the various strands of ethical argumentation, the often ironic and inconclusive discussions act as stimulants to reflection and further enquiry and as invitations to one's own discovery of the value of the opinions expressed.[1] The text is therefore envisioned more as a guide to civic obligations than as a closed system of truth.

How, then, should we view the four highly educated, opinionated, and nameless participants in the discussion? On one level, the individuals in this intellectual encounter are stylized characters, rather like the masked players of the Italian *commedia dell'arte*.[2] The text's *dramatis personae*

---

[1] Platonic dialogues often appear to leave deliberate gaps in logic and arguments, seemingly to invite the reader to fill the gaps with his or her own thoughts.

[2] The setting of the discussion in Italy reflects my own interest in that country. Among the major economies, Italy has had, perhaps, the most extensive and long-running public discourse of combating bribery, from the *mani pulite* ("clean hands") campaigns and judicial investigations into the culture of *Tangentopoli* ("Bribesville") of the 1990s to the anticorruption rhetoric of the *Cinque Stelle* ("Five Star") political movement at the time of this writing. In addition, my four characters in search of an answer to a seemingly absurd question seem to carry echoes of Luigi Pirandello's six characters in search of an author (*Sei personaggi in cerca d'autore*, 1921).

generally remain remarkably faithful to their "masks", with the exception of the classicist, whose insights into the Jewish Bible significantly supplement and amplify the priest's contributions. Indeed, although the discussions are formally chaired by the economist, the classicist's role is central to the flow of the narrative.

It has been suggested that, in the Platonic corpus, "the charm of Socrates lies...in his superiority to the situation"[3] and, to a degree, this judgment may apply to the classicist in our text. He speeds up the discussions in the opening pages when they threaten to get bogged down in lengthy speechmaking; he encourages a focus on practical matters to prevent the discussions spiraling away, like smoke, into abstractions; he prevents the sidelining of the student's contributions in Section Four; and he even rescues the discussion, in the final pages, from a derailment into the red herring of Richard Wagner's music dramas. In general, he steers the narrative in an efficient manner. To use a musical analogy, he tries to limit the participants' wilder chromatic wanderings to focus on the core melodies and harmonies.

The discussions are rich in historical and literary references. Examples of bribes are taken from traditional sources, including the Bible and Plato, supplemented by a range of literary allusions and insights from behavioral economics and critical social theory. The historical and literary examples place bribery in the realm of ethical and artistic traditions of enduring validity: The text therefore invites us to explore bribery in the context of authentically timeless examples of expressions of the human spirit. The voices in the text seem at times to cry out from half-forgotten catacombs of our culture but, as the speakers grope through the mists of history for the primeval sources of our ethical behavior, their discussions resonate with a strikingly modern tone.

---

[3] Voegelin (2000, 63).

A modest critical apparatus supports the discussion to elucidate some of the historical and literary references and allusions and to draw attention to points of interest.[4] The references to various sources do not suggest that the discussion can be reduced to these sources, nor do they imply a necessary commitment by any of the speakers to the viewpoints or metaphysical stances that underpin the references. The annotations serve simply as pointers for further exploration of the themes contained in the discussions.

There is a certain amount of circularity in the text, which is inevitable in an extended conversation. It might therefore seem impossible to isolate certain sections of the discussion without doing violence to the integrity of the whole structure. Indeed, if one tries to draw one particular strand from the discussion, the entire fabric seems to move with the pull. Nonetheless, the text is divided into sections to provide indicators of thematic shifts of emphasis: The section headings aim to be nothing more than signposts and are not intended to act as abrupt stalling points, like the locks that delay and block the flow of water in a large canal.

I present this text to the public in the hope that it might enrich our understanding of bribery. I believe that the discussion's findings have profound implications for public policy. The interactions of the rival ethical viewpoints

---

[4] Biblical references are taken from the New Revised Standard version in the Oxford University Press *New Oxford Annotated Bible*, 3rd ed. (New York: Oxford, 2001), with some amendments, except for quotations from the Jewish Bible when the Jewish Publication Society (JPS) translations available at the time of writing this book seemed preferable. References to the *Catechism of the Catholic Church* are taken from the English-language second edition (New York: Doubleday, 1997). References to Plato provide the Stephanus numbers and translations as they appear in *Plato: Complete Works*, ed. John M. Cooper (Indianapolis: Hackett, 1997). References to Xenophon are taken from the Loeb Classical Library edition, vol. 168 (Cambridge, MA: Harvard University Press, 1923). For Aristotle, Bekker references are provided. All other titles referred to in the notes are listed at the end of the text.

develop in ways too complex and controversial to describe fully in this brief preface, but the economist's arguments for the existence of good, harmless, and ambiguous bribes are not convincingly refuted. If we were to accept the economist's arguments, there would be inevitable implications for the use of "zero tolerance" antibribery policies. Indeed, over time, the arguments of the apologists for some types of bribery might result in bribery as a whole being viewed with increasing legitimacy, or at least with a decreasing sense of illegitimacy.

On the other hand, the discussions also make clear that, notwithstanding the ambiguities and seeming virtues of some transactions on the margins of the vast bulk of bribery, most bribes are without doubt deeply damaging in their social and economic effects. Bribery generally corrupts not only those who give and receive bribes but also the wider society that suffers their consequences.

Perhaps the ultimate question raised by the discussions is where we might strike a balance, in public or institutional policies, in trying to accommodate a fringe of virtuous or ambiguous transactions within the overwhelming mass of harmful bribery. Our four-way discussion may seem to end inconclusively, but it suggests, at a minimum, that ethical matters may be legitimately disputed from a range of perspectives. It also implies that there is no simple model or algorithm that can spit out a "once-size-fits-all" checklist for the ethical assessment of transactions suspected to be bribes. We cannot rely purely on a checklist-compliance approach to bribery.

The application of judgment to bribery transactions therefore appears to be essential in evaluating their harmfulness, and this in turn seems to require an acknowledgment of the complexity of the subject. Both the traditionalists and the radicals in our discussion indicate that solutions to the problem of bribery, especially at its ethical boundaries, tend not to be straightforward. An effective public or institutional policy towards bribery is therefore likely to be nuanced and capable of handling and resolving ambiguities.[5]

I thank Dr. Jeffrey Young of Universal Publishers for valuable guidance on sharpening the structure and clarity of the text. I am grateful also to Professor Michael Power of the London School of Economics and Political Science; Dr. Mark Dooley, biographer of Sir Roger Scruton; Dr. Joan Dubinsky, former Chief Ethics Officer of the United Nations and the International Monetary Fund; and Dr. Amit Chawla of Sharda University for giving generously of their time in reading and commenting on part or all of the text. This does not imply their seal of approval for anything in the book. Even with this collective wisdom and my best efforts, there may remain some errors or omissions, and any infelicities in the text are mine alone. I thank my wife, Abhishikta, in helping me to see the book through to completion.

Falls Church, Virginia
March 2020

---

[5] On the importance of judgment in ethics, see Warnock (1998, 7): "Ethics is a complicated matter. It is partly a matter of general principles, or even rules, like those of manners; but largely a matter of judgement and decision, of reasoning and sentiment, of having the right feeling at the right time, and every time is different."

The Characters and Setting

THE CHARACTERS:

An economist, head of a free-market think tank.
A Roman Catholic priest, lecturer in divinity.
A retired professor of Greek.
A student of French literature.

THE SETTING:

Turin, Italy. Early twenty-first century.

Chapter One
Introduction and Definitions

THE ECONOMIST:

My friends,[6] I'm delighted that we've convened to discuss the ethical dimensions of bribery. I provided you a challenge: to refute my assertion that bribery can be, on occasion, a positive activity with beneficent outcomes. I'm immensely pleased that you've accepted a debate of my claims. And, as we've had several weeks to prepare, I trust that we've all had the chance to do some research or at least to reflect deeply on this topic.[7] So I feel confident in saying that we are well prepared to take on this challenging discussion.

THE PRIEST:

Indeed, it's good that we've had time to ready ourselves for what are bound to be deep, and perhaps difficult, discussions.

---

[6] From the opening words, other than for one or two moments of tension, the tone of the discussions is generally cordial and collegial.

[7] That the participants have been granted a period of prior preparation accounts for the readiness with which they are able to summon a large range of historical and literary examples and allusions.

THE ECONOMIST:

The topic of corruption is an important one, and bribery, we might say, is the quintessential manifestation of corruption.[8] Any justifications of bribery need to be fully explained and not merely explained away. Perhaps it would make sense first to set out our basic arguments in relation to the subject. As we know, we shall be hearing a range of views today. I shall be seeking to justify the use of bribery or, to be more precise, modest-level bribery, in certain circumstances, and at least two among us shall tend to the view that bribery is always inherently wrong.

So, if you allow me to begin, in my capacity as chair, I'd like to set out my position in the following way: To many, if not most, people, bribery is a kind of destructive economic parasitism that undermines social trust and damages individuals. For example, if a police force routinely accepts bribes to let criminals go unpunished, then public confidence in the justice system is damaged, and the victims of crime are betrayed. I accept this for cases of large-scale bribes or bribes that involve serious matters like homicides. But, to pursue my example of the corrupt police official, I consider there to be a legitimate place in some contexts for small-scale bribes on minor matters, like routine traffic offences.

This may seem provocative, but I'm an economist, and I'm interested in the operation of markets. Small-scale bribes clear markets quickly and promote economic efficiency. Their effect can be likened to the way oil lubricates otherwise inefficient economic and social machinery. I'd even go further and argue that bribery is an unavoidable feature of the human condition. All around the world we see cultures of

---

[8] See Anechiarico and Jacobs (1996, 4). Also, Noonan (1984, xvi) informs us that "treason and bribery are the [only] two crimes named in the Constitution" of the United States.

exchange and reciprocity. Gifts[9] and bribes are embedded in the networks of trust that bind communities together. In my view, gift-giving may be may be envisioned as a distillation of social knowledge that is deeper than rational, articulable knowledge. Gifts and bribes define and reinforce interpersonal arrangements, acting as shortcuts to a harmony of human and economic needs.

THE PRIEST:

Interesting. Please continue.

THE ECONOMIST:

A gift or a bribe can be seen as a problem-solving mechanism in the context of social cooperation and competition. People in markets cooperate and compete, and gifts can be used for both these purposes in a nonviolent way. A gift implants reconciliation in the fabric of society. Just as the price mechanism distils social knowledge and crystallizes a massive quantity of information to assist us in exchange transactions, so bribery supplements the rational, articulable knowledge that is expressed in such economic signals. Gifts and bribes help us to discharge our obligations.

The small bribe, we may therefore say, is a problem-solving mechanism that arises naturally from the necessities of human demands in a market. It provides solutions to economic problems in the manner of the operations of the "invisible hand" of the price mechanism in a Hayekian

---

[9] The economist uses the terms "gift" and "bribe" fairly interchangeably in his opening comments. This, perhaps, plays a part in the subsequent suggestion by the classicist that the participants should define bribery before continuing the discussions. In Section Five, the economist differentiates more carefully between the two terms.

spontaneous order.[10] And, if we accept this view, attempts to eradicate bribery are bound to fail. And we all know—do we not?—that bribery is ineradicable. The giving of gifts to influence others is as old as human social intercourse. As long as bribery is kept within reasonable parameters, such as making a legitimate transaction move faster, bribery can be a means of social order, not disorder.

THE STUDENT:

I think you underestimate the impact of bribery on power relations and on the consolidation of the power of economic elites. The incentives created by bribery are likely to be misaligned to the common interest and certainly injurious to minority and marginalized groups. Bribes reinforce established and illegitimate hierarchies of social power.

THE ECONOMIST:

I see that the spirit of the *soixante-huitards*[11] is with us today. But you make a fair point, and you express it well. It demands a response. We need to explore this topic in some depth.

THE CLASSICIST:

And I would also add my immediate reaction to your words, which is that bribery's longevity as part of the human

---

[10] In his opening comments, the economist's references to F.A. Hayek (1899–1992) and the "invisible hand" of Adam Smith (1723–1790) suggest that his views—or at least the starting point for his analysis—are based on the advocacy of free markets arising from noncoercive association in a self-regulating society, as opposed to both private monopolies and top-down, public sector planning systems of economic allocation.

[11] The *soixante-huitards* are those who took part in, or who have drawn inspiration from, the revolutionary politics of the May 1968 student uprising in Paris.

condition, like greed, is no indication of desirability. It seems to me that bribery flourishes when markets are not free in the Hayekian sense. Bribes are distortions and parodies of transactions arising from free association. They reflect market pathologies. They interfere with the price mechanism. Overall, I see bribes as acts of moral, as well as economic, corruption.

THE PRIEST:

I agree.

THE CLASSICIST:

So, as far as I'm concerned, I see bribes as perversions of the Hayekian spontaneous order. It's the intransigent, rent-seeking[12] bureaucrat, the bullying monopolist, and the gangster who thrive on bribery. As for your analogy with Adam Smith's "invisible hand", I'd say that bribery is a disease that cripples this hand. It thrives especially in agency contexts in which intermediaries subvert economic transactions.[13]

THE ECONOMIST:

Your points of view are well taken, though I would dispute some of them. I touched briefly on the notion of the ends

---

[12] With the term "rent-seeking", the classicist refers to an exploitation of bureaucratic power to accrue income above that established by market conditions. Søreide (2014, 2) defines rent-seeking as "efforts to manipulate the social or political environment to obtain...benefits [gained by market distortions], rather than investing time and/or money in productive work and creating new wealth". The concept of the "rent-seeking" bureaucrat was developed by the "Virginia School" of public choice theory, notably in the work of James Buchanan (1919–2013) and Gordon Tullock (1922–2014). See Tullock (2005).

[13] On bribery as an agency problem, in which bribery subverts the relationship between a principal (including the public) and an agent (the bureaucrat), see Klitgaard (1988, passim) and Nichols (2015, 657).

justifying the means.[14] The ramifications of bribes may have an impact on how we judge them. We all accept, I'm sure, that there is a distinction between serious lies and harmless "white lies". So there is, perhaps, a small, permissible bribery that we may dislike but tolerate, which contrasts with the unacceptable, gargantuan bribery schemes of the modern kleptocratic state.[15]

THE CLASSICIST:

Well, here we are in Italy, which has been damaged more than most European countries by large-scale corruption, including bribery. At this point, please allow me to raise a concern. The economic arguments we've talked about have been fascinating and provocative. But I fear that we've already plunged too quickly into deep, dangerous waters, and there is a risk that our discussions will proceed in a disorderly manner. I propose that we take a step backwards and start by defining "bribery". It will serve us well to have a common understanding of what we're discussing. And I suggest that we follow our definition by proceeding first with what

---

[14] The economist shall discuss the consequentalist approach to bribery in greater detail in Section Five.

[15] A differentiation between minor and major bribery is common in, and perhaps central to, concepts of bribery. Small "facilitating payments" intended to induce an official simply to perform his or her established duties, without additional favors, are differentiated from bribes in the Foreign Corrupt Practices Act of 1977 (and its amendments). The Knapp Commission, set up in 1970 to investigate police corruption in New York following the whistleblowing disclosures by Frank Serpico, used interesting metaphors in its 1972 report, distinguishing between the actions of "grass eaters" and "meat eaters". The former referred to those involved in petty, opportunistic corruption and the latter to those who undertook major, premeditated corruption (Brioschi, 2017, 162). See also Ariely (2008, 196ff) for a discussion of the behavioral differences between opportunistic criminals and career criminals. From a legal perspective, the common law maxim of de minimis non curat lex (the law does not concern itself with trivialities) is relevant to this concept.

we may call the traditionalist arguments of those among us who consider bribery to be wrong. These views, it seems to me, rest in a fusion of biblical and secular concepts, the latter originating in ancient Greece. One does not need to be Jewish or Christian to appreciate biblical wisdom. Similarly, it is not necessary to be a committed Platonist or a devotee of Aristotle to gain insights from the Greeks.

THE STUDENT:

Seriously? I agree to starting with a definition of bribery. But you're asking us to use the Bible and the Greeks as our starting point? Why should we put the clock back, so to speak, in our discussions?

THE CLASSICIST:

Please bear with me. All of us who sit around this table today are, to a greater or lesser degree, products of the biblical and Greek cultures that, together, have defined Western civilization. Some prefer Jerusalem to Athens. Others favor Athens. Some repudiate both. But we all live in the shadow of this dual heritage. And, as far as I'm concerned, the onus of proof in our discussion rests with the apologists for bribery. So let us first define bribery and then set out traditional views of the harmfulness of bribery that are derived, as I say, from a combination of Jerusalem and Athens, and then we can move on to modern challenges to those views. In this way, I think we would maximize the value of our discussion.

THE ECONOMIST:

That's alright. I've no objection to your proposal. I think we may all agree on the necessity of defining bribery. We may then consider the conservative and traditionalist views of bribery before we proceed to engage with modern concepts.

THE PRIEST:

This approach makes sense. Irrespective of any religious commitment, we're living over a vast, subterranean reservoir of Judeo-Christian and Hellenic culture that continues to nurture us. Let's set out this cultural context before we hear any attempts to counter it, whether from radical free market economics or radical postmodernism.

THE STUDENT:

Well, I tend to keep away from metaphysical matters. I was always told that things divine are not for mortals to know! But it seems logical to set out any discredited grand narratives[16] before we demolish them.

THE CLASSICIST:

(Laughs). That remains to be seen, though I've awarded marks to my students for such comments in the past.

THE ECONOMIST:

Well then, let me start by offering a pithy description of bribery that may set us in the right direction. I'd describe bribery as "influence-peddling gift-giving". Let's use this as a springboard for our definition.

---

[16] An allusion to the postmodernist mistrust of overarching, definitive discourses that purport to provide exhaustive descriptions and legitimizations of aspects of the human condition. The term "grand narrative" (or, frequently, meta-narrative) is particularly associated with Jean-François Lyotard (1924–1998).

THE PRIEST:

Fair enough. I think it's a good starting point for us to refine and chisel our definition into a workable shape. My first comment is that a gift or bribe can take many forms. A bribe might simply be an envelope stuffed with cash, an asset like a fancy watch, or a service of some kind. It might be as simple as a meal, a bottle of whiskey, or some form of hospitality. It might even involve the non-performance of a service: Take, for example, a tax official who accepts a promotion in return for not processing an individual's tax return.

THE STUDENT:

I agree that the concept of the influence-peddling gift is wide, but I think this very wideness is helpful to our discussions. As you've said, bribery isn't limited only to money transactions. Bribery can also take place in the form of sexual services—we all know that big business uses sex workers to gratify individuals so they will serve its interests. A customer in two minds about entering into a big contract? Provide him with a sexual service, with all the exploitation that this implies, and you can bend him to your will. In cases like this, we can see how bribery reinforces inequalities and exploitation.

THE CLASSICIST:

We're on a good track. But I think we need to draw a line between a gift that's simply a gift and a gift that's a bribe. If I offer my children an appealing vacation if they achieve high school grades, that surely isn't a bribe. It's simply an inducement to encourage good behavior. On the other hand, if I offer my children a vacation if they steal or somehow improperly obtain in advance the answers to their test papers, that would be a bribe because it would encourage bad behavior.

THE ECONOMIST:

Exactly. That's why my definition includes the term "influence-peddling". This is intended in a pejorative sense. We're not talking about gifts given through generosity, with no expectation of reward. It all comes down to intentions and consequences. A bribe is a gift that's intended to trigger a certain type of behavior. You can't blame a bottle of whiskey if it's used for malign purposes: The whiskey itself is neutral, but how it's used by others determines if it becomes a channel for a gift or a bribe.[17]

THE PRIEST:

I agree with you. But if, as you seem to be saying, a bribe is something that encourages bad behavior, then why defend bribery? Are you engaged in some kind of antinomian[18] crusade?

THE ECONOMIST:

(Laughs). Not at all. I don't deny that bribery can have bad, even terrible, consequences. My argument is that we can live with minor bribes—let us call them economic "white lies"—in the interest of the greater good.

---

[17] The distinction in ethical theory between consequentialism (the view that the morality of an act is based on its consequences) and the deontological view that an act is intrinsically moral or immoral (irrespective, or largely irrespective, of its consequences) is discussed only briefly here, but it is developed in greater detail in Sections Four and Five.

[18] The priest is clearly not using the term antinomian in the purely Christian sense of the transgression of Old Testament moral codes owing to the belief that salvation is based on faith alone, rather than on action. He is using the term in the broader sense of liberation from established or traditional codes of conduct.

THE PRIEST:

The greater good?

THE ECONOMIST:

Absolutely. As I tried to say earlier, if we seek moral perfection in every one of our transactions,[19] our markets will simply seize up. But size matters. I'm not talking of large-scale bribery that lets killers off the hook or that ruins people's livelihoods. I'm talking of minor infractions, like turning a blind eye to a parking ticket. So I'd like to propose a modification to my definition. I'd like the add the term "small-scale" to the definition.[20] Do you agree that it makes sense to talk about "influence-peddling, small-scale gifts"?

THE CLASSICIST:

I'm not sure about that. A revised definition along those lines makes it seem that what matters is the scale of the bribe. But shouldn't we be addressing more than just the size of a transaction? Shouldn't we also consider the very nature of a bribe, as well as the intentions behind it, in addition to its consequences? I may offer a bribe of small monetary value, but it may be enough to trigger a horrendous outcome, like allowing a killer to evade justice. So we shouldn't fixate on the size of a bribe.

---

[19] Compare the notion of moral perfectionism in Christian theology (in which an exaggeratedly scrupulous conscience can distort moral judgment and even have evil consequences), which is developed towards the end of Section Two.

[20] On the topic of the size of a gift or bribe, Noonan (1984, 91) suggests that "to call...baksheesh corrupt would be to confuse a tip and a bribe".

THE PRIEST:

I concur.

THE ECONOMIST:

Understood. I don't disagree with you, in terms of the definition at least. I was perhaps a little sloppy in placing my adjective in the middle of the definition. In order to cover both the size of the bribe and the magnitude of its outcomes, let me add the word "minor" at the beginning of the definition, as follows: "minor, influence-peddling gift-giving."

THE CLASSICIST:

Good. For me, this will do, at this stage. The addition of the word "minor" sits better this way.

THE STUDENT:

There's a lot more that needs to be done to make the definition workable. For example, who will define what is minor and acceptable or large and unacceptable? There's no obvious way to measure this. Concrete forms of bribery may be trickier to handle than abstract principles.

THE CLASSICIST:

For sure, you're right. But I'm hoping that our discussions will cast light on such matters. I think that, as a working definition for use as a starting point, the new phrasing is an enhancement. And if you don't object, I'd like to take another step and eliminate the notion of giving bribes, as specified in the definition. Can't accepting a bribe be just as bad as offering one? If I'm offered a bribe to, let's say, alter a student's grades, and I accept it, am I not just as guilty as the person who offered the bribe?

THE STUDENT:

Certainly. I'd say that both parties are equally culpable under such circumstances.

THE CLASSICIST:

Then let's modify the definition again to eliminate the reference to giving. Both giving and accepting bribes should be covered by our discussions. So we might say that bribery, as we shall discuss it here, deals with "minor, influence-peddling gifts".

THE STUDENT:

I can accept this.

THE ECONOMIST:

Then let's take stock of where we are. By talking of gifts, we're not restricting ourselves to monetary transactions. And we're dealing only with gifts intended to elicit a *quid pro quo* of some kind. We'll discuss not only the offering of bribes but also their acceptance. I'm sure we could refine the definition in a lot more detail, but in the interests of time, and with an eye to keeping the definition short, this seems to me to be a good starting point.

THE PRIEST:

Wait a minute, please. I don't dispute the need to move on, but I don't think we've yet exhausted our review of the definition.

What about the role of freedom and self-responsibility? If I offer or accept a bribe with a gun pointed to my head, then surely I can't be held guilty of bribery?

THE ECONOMIST:

You're opening up deep questions. They're not invalid, but I wonder if they really affect a definition that will suit our purposes.

THE PRIEST:

What do you mean?

THE ECONOMIST:

Well, I accept the point about coercion. If a police official points a gun to my head while he solicits a bribe, then I'd be foolish not to pay up.[21] My freedom of action would obviously be constrained in such a case. But rather than amend the definition, can we not simply proceed on the understanding that we're discussing noncoercive bribery?

THE STUDENT:

Allow me to offer a word of caution here. When we talk of coercion, we're not simply talking about putting a gun to someone's head. Many of us are coerced by less visible factors, like economic and social exploitation. If I'm a police official in a poor country, and I have a starving family, then is it wrong for me to solicit bribes to put food on the table for my children? These considerations are at the heart of some of the arguments I wish to advance in our discussions. But I

---

[21] Velasquez (2012, 488) discusses the concept that it is not necessarily morally wrong to comply with the demands of an extortionist, even when this involves a bribe.

think it'll be difficult to incorporate this into our definition as it's phrased right now.

THE CLASSICIST:

You're probably right. In terms of coercion in bribery, and the virtue, or otherwise, of bribes, I propose that we let these emerge from our discussions rather than try to pre-empt the outcomes of the discussions by pointing the definition in a particular direction.

THE PRIEST:

Can you remind me again of the current wording of our definition?

THE ECONOMIST:

Our most recent definition is that bribery consists of "minor, influence-peddling gifts".[22] This is very succinct, and a lot more could be added. For example, what about the relationship of bribery to legality? What about the clash of public and private interests that lies at the heart of so much bribery? I'm aware that our current definition doesn't capture all possible nuances of the topic, but I think it's adequate as a springboard for discussion.

---

[22] "Minor, influence-peddling gifts." Compare other definitions of bribery: Noonan (1984, xi and 697) provides pithy definitions of a bribe as "an inducement improperly influencing the performance of a public function meant to be gratuitously exercised" and "any inducement given to alter conduct that would be naturally otherwise". Søreide (2014, 1) suggests that at the heart of a bribe is "a decision 'sold' to benefit the briber, while the bribe payment compensates for the decision maker's risks and moral cost of betraying the institution". On corruption in general, Rose-Ackerman (1999, 91) offers the succinct definition of "the misuse of public power for private gain".

THE PRIEST:

I'm not sure we should leave our definition half baked, so to speak. There's so much more to add.

THE CLASSICIST:

I can sense your dissatisfaction. And, frankly, I share it to an extent. I'd also like to add some things to the definition. But, despite its pithiness, I think it can serve us well as a starting point for our analysis. Let me propose that we take this definition forward and, perhaps, we can revise it in the light of our discussions, maybe as a way to conclude our analysis.[23]

THE STUDENT:

I like your suggestion.

THE PRIEST:

Then, as we agreed, let's take a look at what the Bible tells us about bribery.

---

[23] The participants' frustrated search for an initial definition of bribery reflects, perhaps, the aporetic (inconclusive) search for definitions in some of Plato's shorter dialogues, examples of which include the inconclusive search for a definition of "piety" in *Euthyphro* and a similarly frustrated search for a definition of "courage" in *Laches*. In contrast, in the present text, the effect of the initial aporia is not simply frustrated abandonment of the analysis but rather a stimulus to further investigation, in a manner similar to some of Plato's larger works, notably in the searches for definitions of "rhetoric" in *Gorgias* and of "justice" in the *Republic* (without necessarily reaching an entirely conclusive definition in the latter cases). As Szlezák (1999, 127) has reminded us, the aporia itself can be meaningful and might even possess educative value: "...aporetic dialogues do not simply revel in ambivalences but can be very unambiguous in their denial of whatever is wrong and mistaken."

Chapter Two
Bribery in the Bible

THE STUDENT:

So, as you've proposed, now seems to be the moment for us to dash impetuously to the protective sanctuary of religion. But I think we should be cautious about accepting any need for faith to drive our interpretations.[24]

THE CLASSICIST:

Well, I wouldn't put our discussions in quite those terms. To me, it seems appropriate to start our investigations with a glance at the roots of our ethical system. Even if, as I suspect, you'll relish the opportunity to attack those roots, it's surely crucial to set them out as a basis for our analysis.

THE PRIEST:

I fully agree. It doesn't require faith in Christ to understand biblical morality.

---

[24] The student appears to be alluding to the Anselmian maxim *credo ut intelligam*, by which religious faith is a prerequisite to understanding.

THE STUDENT:

Gentlemen, don't get me wrong. It's not that I wish to rock the boat for its own sake. I'll have plenty to say in due course about our alleged civilizational roots. So let's proceed as you suggest, but in the awareness that religious societies tend to be more corrupt than secular societies and also with the recognition that we are dealing with a Eurocentric, patriarchal superstition as the launching pad for our discussions.

THE PRIEST:

Steady on, please! I'm not sure it's necessarily true that religious societies are more corrupt than secular societies.[25] And as a member of the Catholic Church, I should remind you that "catholic" means universal. The message of Christ is the opposite of Eurocentric.

THE ECONOMIST:

Let's not get ahead of ourselves. We'll have ample opportunity to discuss such matters in the course of our discussions. Please, for now, let's review what the Bible has to say about bribery. Subsequently, we can undertake our discussions and analysis in a more systematic manner.

THE PRIEST:

I'll begin, then, by saying that biblical morality is all encompassing. This is what I always impress on my students.

---

[25] Research has indicated that the student may be correct on this matter. For example, Senior (2006, 163–164) described as "disheartening" the findings of his research that "high overt religiosity, far from repressing corruption, seems to make it more common". However, correlation is not causation and other secondary factors may be at play—including the degree of conformity to social authoritarianism and a weak differentiation between the public and private spheres—which may be more pronounced in societies with highly traditional religious beliefs.

From the Ten Commandments to the Sermon on the Mount, the Bible provides the essence of everything we need to know in order to lead an ethical life. These ethical principles apply to the daily problems we all face. Therefore, although bribery is not one of the major topics in the Bible, despite some striking examples, the biblical approach to bribery can be inferred from its wider moral framework.

So to repeat: Bribery should be understood within the overall biblical message on how to treat others, on how to avoid corruption of various kinds, and on how to resist greed. Now it's especially true that, in the New Testament, bribery is not a significant topic. The major exception, as we all know, is the bribery of Judas with thirty pieces of silver...

THE CLASSICIST:

Please excuse my interruption. With your permission, I'd like to ask you all to listen to a suggestion before we continue because I believe it may have a bearing on our discussions.[26] Because of my Jewish background, I took advantage of the preparation time to review in depth what the Jewish Bible has to say about bribery. Of course, in terms of terminology, for me the Jewish Bible is by no means an Old Testament: It is very much a living document, so I shall not be using the term "Old Testament".

THE PRIEST:

Of course, and I understand. By referring to the Old Testament, I did not mean to make any dogmatic assertion. It's merely the conventional Christian term for the Jewish Bible.

---

[26] As in Section One, it is the classicist who alters the broad trajectory of the discussion. In this case, we see an exception to the pattern of the discussion's participants remaining close to their designations as economist, priest, radical student, and classicist. The classicist's insights into the Jewish Bible significantly amplify the priest's subsequent discussions of the New Testament.

THE CLASSICIST:

Absolutely. You intended no offense, and none was taken. So allow me to pursue my thoughts along the lines that the relationships between the Jewish Bible and the New Testament are not symmetrical.

THE ECONOMIST:

What do you mean? I don't understand.

THE CLASSICIST:

My point is that the New Testament makes little sense without the Jewish Bible that precedes it. Christians understand the New Testament as building on, affirming, or in some way completing the Jewish Bible. Christian Bibles have their "Old" and "New" Testaments to sequentially set out the basis for faith. In contrast, the Jewish Bible stands alone and makes sense entirely on its own terms, without the New Testament. Am I being clear? Is this controversial?

THE PRIEST:

No, it's not controversial. You're right. Christianity has obviously developed into a different religion, distinct from Judaism, but it grew out of the Jewish faith like a branch grows out of a tree. Various Christian traditions differ on the precise nature of the relationship, but there is no question that, in overall terms, the relationship is as you describe.[27]

---

[27] The priest does not mention the Marcionites, an early Christian movement that was rejected and declared heretical by what became orthodox Christianity. The New Testament did not yet exist in the time of Marcion (approximately 85–160), but Marcion and his followers contributed to the debates over what would comprise the New Testament by advocating that Christians totally sever their theology (and writings) from the Jewish tradition, including the Jewish Bible. See Ehrman (2003, 103–109).

I see the Old and New Testaments as inextricably interrelated, with the New Testament logically following from the earlier Jewish Bible and affirming its contents. Yet, on the other hand, as you've said, the Jews don't need the New Testament because their Bible is self-contained. So yes, I agree with you. Definitely.

THE CLASSICIST:

I'm glad we can agree on this as our starting point. This has no implications, positive or negative, on our faith commitments. It's simply a statement of fact. It therefore follows—does it not?—that because the New Testament is intended to build on the Jewish Bible, it tends not to repeat many of the contents of the Jewish Bible. The Christian Bible is rich in references and allusions to parts of the Jewish Bible, making connections and elaborating on certain matters and so on, but it doesn't need to repeat verbatim large passages of the Jewish Bible. There is an assumption that the reader is already familiar with the Jewish Bible, and so the New Testament sits like a statue on top of an older pedestal. Are we agreed?

THE PRIEST:

True. The assumptions underpinning the New Testament are as you say.

THE ECONOMIST:

What you say makes sense.

THE CLASSICIST:

Then we can agree that the New Testament overtly builds on the contents of the Jewish Bible for the theological purpose of claiming continuity with the Jewish tradition. Many of the underlying assumptions already set out in the Jewish Bible are therefore not explicitly restated in the New Testament. It therefore follows, I would argue, that the New Testament doesn't address bribery in depth because the Jewish Bible has already made this topic profoundly clear. So, if you permit, I'd like to first set out some of the basic principles contained in the Jewish Bible in relation to bribery, and then we can proceed to discuss the New Testament.

THE PRIEST:

Your approach strikes me as reasonable and uncontroversial. I can accept it. The Jewish Bible preceded the New Testament not only chronologically but also, as we have agreed, theologically and thematically. I've no objection to you continuing the discussion in this manner.

THE STUDENT:

You're all well aware of my views on religion. But I don't have a problem with your proposed approach. Now I think it's time for us to move on, to hear some concrete examples of biblical morality when it comes to bribery.

THE CLASSICIST:

Alright. As we've reached agreement on this, I shall begin to discuss specific examples. You may be surprised to learn that the Jewish Bible is more nuanced on bribery than you may have imagined. Nonetheless, and perhaps unexpectedly, the biblical starting point is that bribery is ethically unacceptable.

In the Mosaic Law, references to bribery relate mainly to judges, and there is, therefore, an emphasis on integrity in the administration of justice. In *Exodus*, the judges are told the following: "Do not take bribes, for bribes blind the clear-sighted and upset the pleas of those who are in the right."[28] This condemnation of bribery is unequivocal, and it emphasizes the negative consequences of bribery. Bribes distort judgment and subvert justice. I mention, as an aside, that we'll also be discussing the relationship of justice to bribery when we move on to the classical Greek virtues later.

The strong condemnation of bribery in *Exodus* is reinforced in *Deuteronomy*: "You shall not judge unfairly; you shall show no partiality; you shall not take bribes, for bribes blind the eyes of the discerning and upset the plea of the just."[29] And there is a particularly strong condemnation for bribery that is related to cases of unjustified killing: "Cursed be he who accepts a bribe in the case of a murder of an innocent person."[30] When an innocent life is at stake, a divine curse awaits the person who accepts a bribe. This is strong stuff; I think you will agree.

THE ECONOMIST:

Yes, these are unambiguously strong condemnations. But you say that these references are relevant mainly to the formal administration of justice. Is there any extrapolation of bribery beyond the law courts to the general population as a whole?

THE CLASSICIST:

So far, I've set out only some initial, limited references to bribery in the Bible. There are many more references, with wider applications. There's even an astonishing passage in which

---

[28] *Exodus* 23:8. In this sentence Sarna (1991, 143) has drawn attention to the fact that the "Hebrew syntax highlights the severity of the offense by placing 'bribe' in the emphatic initial position".

[29] *Deuteronomy* 16:19.

[30] *Deuteronomy* 27:25.

God is described anthropomorphically as a ruler who "takes no bribe".[31] The implications of this, if we reflect carefully, are quite staggering. The maintenance of integrity in the administration of justice, we are told, amounts to the following of godly virtue. In other words, the avoidance of bribery is a form of *imitatio dei*.[32] Just as we are made in God's image, so we are encouraged to behave like God, too.

THE PRIEST:

It's hard to exaggerate the strength of this ethical condemnation.

THE CLASSICIST:

Exactly. This is no minor law or suggested guidance. It's no mystical allegory. Rather, it's intrinsic to the concept of a just society. Jewish law is notably down-to-earth, and it focuses very much on the realities of life in the here and now.[33] And none of the building blocks of a just society can be discarded without undermining the whole of society.

Later in the Bible, the negative portrayal of bribery continues. What has always struck me is the fact that so many of the prophets were infuriated by and railed against bribery.[34] This suggests that the practice was a widespread form of corruption in society in biblical times, obviously to an extent

---

[31] *Deuteronomy* 10:17–18.

[32] *Imitatio dei:* the imitation of God, i.e. a person's obligation to emulate God's behavior.

[33] As Jonathan Sacks has expressed this concept: "[A]t the highest levels of mysticism, God is to be found in the innermost depths of the human soul, but God is equally to be found in the public square and in the structures of society: the market-place, the corridors of power, and the courts of law" (Sacks, 2010, 177).

[34] See, for example, *Ezekiel* 22:12, *Isaiah* 1:23, 5:23, and 33:15, and *Micah* 3:11.

that was sufficient to warrant the prophets' anger. After all, if bribery wasn't a big deal, why would the prophets repeatedly condemn it in such strong terms?

THE PRIEST:

You've certainly done our discussions a favor by setting out how the Jewish biblical texts condemn bribery. And there's more, too. In one of the psalms, for example, it says that the man who will "never be shaken" includes he who has never "accepted a bribe against the innocent".[35] In another psalm, there is a prayer for divine justice and a request not to be swept along with those whose "hands are full of bribes".[36] And Job's visitor Eliphaz says, in his discussion of the fate of the wicked, that "fire consumes the tents of the briber".[37] Without doubt, I would say, all givers and receivers of bribes, and not just those involved in the formal administration of justice, are portrayed as evildoers.

THE CLASSICIST:

It's also worth mentioning that the cases of bribery recorded in the biblical narratives tend to lead to negative outcomes. Delilah's betrayal of Samson was, in part, a result of bribery.[38] And in Esther,[39] Haman bribes King Ahasuerus with ten thousand talents of silver in an attempt to obtain permission to murder the Jewish population in Persia. There is

---

[35] *Psalm* 15:5.

[36] *Psalm* 26:10.

[37] *Job* 15:34. See also Job's earlier comments in 6:22–23.

[38] "The lords of the Philistines went up to her [Delilah] and said, 'Coax him and find out what makes him so strong, and how we can overpower him, tie him up, and make him helpless; and we'll each give you eleven hundred shekels of silver'" (*Judges* 16:5). The narrative is silent about Delilah's subsequent fate after she accepts the bribe.

[39] *Esther* 3:9.

some ambiguity over whether King Ahasuerus refused the bribe: In any case, he allowed Haman to try to implement his genocide.

I'll give a final example. The sons of Samuel "did not follow in his [God's] ways; they were bent on gain, they accepted bribes, and they subverted justice".[40] The consequences of the bribery of Samuel's sons were far reaching, as it contributed to a gathering of the elders for the purpose of ending the rule of the judges and opening the door to the establishment of a monarchy.[41]

THE STUDENT:

I think you've done an admirable job. It's clear that the Jewish Bible took a dim view of bribery. But let's not get overwhelmed with details. The overall point is made and well taken. I think we should move on.

THE CLASSICIST:

Very well. If you're satisfied with the evidence I've put forward so far, I don't think there's a need for me to continue with any more examples of this type.[42] I would add, however, that the

---

[40] I *Samuel* 8:3.

[41] I *Samuel* 8:3–22. It was hoped that the change of governance arrangements would put an end to abuses of power and corrupt practices like bribery. In this case, the consequences of reforming a culture of bribery were so far-reaching that they led to, or contributed significantly to, "regime change", with the establishment of the monarchy.

[42] Perhaps the classicist had in mind two more striking examples of bribery recorded in the Jewish Bible. The first is that of Asa, the third king of Judah, in his struggles against King Baasha of Israel: "Asa took all the silver and gold that remained in the treasuries of the House of the Lord, as well as the treasuries of the royal palace, and he entrusted them to his officials. King Asa sent them to King Ben-hadad son of Tabrimmon son of Hezion of Aram, who resided in Damascus, with this message: 'There is a pact between you and me, and between your father and my father.

Jewish Oral Law seems to take an even stricter approach to bribery than is found in the Bible. For example, as part of a detailed discussion of the ethics of fees and gifts in legal proceedings, the Talmud records the Rabbinic authorities' comments that a bribe may not be taken even if the purpose is ostensibly desirable, such as acquitting the innocent or condemning the guilty.[43]

THE PRIEST:

That's highly interesting. So both the Jewish Bible and the Talmud tell us that bribery is categorically immoral, whatever the consequences of the bribe. Before we move to a discussion of the New Testament, I think it's fair to say that the apologists for bribery can find little or no support or justifications in the Jewish biblical texts. And so let's...

I therefore send you a gift of silver and gold: Go and break your pact with King Baasha of Israel, so that he may withdraw from me'" (1 *Kings* 15:18–19). This monetary bribe to the Aramean king was successful in that it led to a shift of alliances that benefitted Asa. However, the tribes of Dan and Naphtali fell under the political domination of the Arameans as a consequence. Hanani the Seer admonished Asa, much to Asa's annoyance, for relying on his bribe-induced alliance rather than on God (2 *Chronicles* 16:7–10). Despite the initial successes of Asa's reign, and his initial reliance on God that gave him outstanding military victories, Asa's reign ended in sickness, conflict, and the oppression of his own people. This decline appears to have been inextricably linked to his bribery of a pagan king and his related mistreatment of Hanani. The second example is King Ahaz of Judah's bribery of foreign allies for military and political assistance: "Ahaz took the gold and silver that were on hand in the House of the Lord and in the treasuries of the Royal Palace and sent them as a gift to the king of Assyria" (2 *Kings* 16:8). Ahaz's bribes and political maneuvering were able to preserve Judah from the immediate threats of invasion and military expeditions by his neighbors, but the consequences of Assyrian power ultimately led to the disappearance of the northern kingdom and the reduction of Judah to a vassal state. In both these examples, the bribes may have led to short-term benefits but, ultimately, they triggered negative, longer-term outcomes.

[43] *Kethuboth* 105a. Cohen (1932, 221) describes this as a "demand for the strictest justice".

THE CLASSICIST:

Not so fast, please. The Jewish Bible does indeed condemn the kind of bribery that subverts justice, and it does so in harsh terms. But we should remember that gift-giving is a social practice. Not all gifts are bribes, and this is an important distinction to maintain, especially in a culture like that of the Middle East, where gifts and reciprocity are woven into the fabric of the culture.[44] The most common Hebrew word for "bribe" in the Bible is *shoḥad,*[45] which can also mean "gift", depending on the situation. And this touches the heart of our problem: When does a gift become a bribe?[46]

THE STUDENT:

Well, when does it?

THE CLASSICIST:

Basically, judgment is required. The biblical critique of bribery is tempered by wisdom. In biblical terms, we may say it is tempered by Solomonic wisdom.

THE STUDENT:

What do you mean?

---

[44] On the cultural significance of gift-giving, consider the state of near panic that engulfs Saul when, as he approaches Samuel, he realizes that he has no gift to offer (1 *Samuel* 9:5–8).

[45] In the Bible, the Hebrew noun *shoḥad,* שוחד, can be translated as gift, offering, or bribe, depending on the circumstances. (In the Septuagint, *dōron,* δῶρον, was the Greek translation of שוחד).

[46] As Rose-Ackerman (1999, 92) puts it: "The difficulty of distinguishing gifts from bribes has its roots in their fundamental similarity." The sometimes fraught distinction between a gift and a bribe is central to the following discussions.

THE CLASSICIST:

The biblical critique of bribery is tempered in the book of *Proverbs*. According to tradition, Solomon was the author of *Proverbs*.[47]

THE STUDENT:

Do you seriously want us to believe that Solomon personally authored the biblical proverbs? It's well known that the false attribution of ancient texts was a means of trying to boost their legitimacy.

THE CLASSICIST:

I don't wish right now to get into the disputes over pseudepigraphy.[48] All I'm saying is that tradition holds Solomon to be the author of *Proverbs* and, rightly or wrongly, this is how matters are perceived by many. And what Solomon, or whoever wrote in his name, had to say about gift-giving was very interesting.

THE ECONOMIST:

Tell us, please.

THE CLASSICIST:

We're told that "a man's gift eases his way and gives him access to the great".[49] This warrants our close attention.

---

[47] A *midrash* (ancient biblical commentary) indicates that *Proverbs* was one of three biblical books ascribed to Solomon at various stages of his life—the eroticism of the *Song of Songs* belonged to his youth, the wisdom of *Proverbs* to his middle age, and the reflections on the vanities of life in *Ecclesiastes* to his old age (*Song of Songs Rabbah* I.1, section 10, Soncino edition, London, 3rd ed. 1983).

[48] The false ascription of authorship to literary texts.

[49] *Proverbs* 18:16.

There's no sense of condemnation here. What this implies is that a gift or small bribe made simply to gain access to an official may be permitted, provided that the intention is not to subvert justice.

THE ECONOMIST:

That's not a million miles away from what I was trying to convey in my opening remarks. Minor bribes that are not intended to subvert justice, but simply to oil the machinery of a system of power, may be acceptable. This is highly interesting.

THE CLASSICIST:

Proverbs also tells us that "a gift in secret subdues anger, a present in private, fierce rage".[50] Again, there is no hint of condemnation. Here we seem to be dealing with a bribe that placates an angry official who considers himself to have been wronged. Again, as I understand it, the implication is that a bribe may be acceptable if the underlying intentions are honorable and the consequences are not bad.

Let me make this point clear by contrasting it with yet another quotation from *Proverbs*: "The wicked man draws a bribe out of his bosom to pervert the course of justice."[51] In this case, there is a clear condemnation of the bribe, linked to the subversion of justice, which is the direct consequence of the bribe. What I conclude from all this is that the author of *Proverbs* is telling us that the nature and consequences of gifts determine their moral value.

---

[50] *Proverbs* 21:14.
[51] *Proverbs* 17:23.

THE PRIEST:

Then correct me if I speak in error, but it seems to me that the book of *Proverbs* does not condemn gift-giving per se, but only the abuse of gift-giving.

THE CLASSICIST:

Precisely.

THE PRIEST:

I did in fact come up with another reference to gifts among the proverbs: "A bribe seems like a charm to him who uses it; he succeeds at every turn."[52] This appears to me to be a little ambiguous. It shows that the proverbs require careful reflection. In this case, I sense that the proverb is alluding to the damaging effects of bribery on individuals who rely on bribery to negotiate their way through life. It's possibly about self-deception.

THE CLASSICIST:

I think you're right. The proverb you've just quoted suggests that bribes may open doors, especially in the short term, but ultimately bribery is a destructive activity.[53]

THE PRIEST:

But it's ambiguous.

---

[52] *Proverbs* 17:8.

[53] The classicist might have compared the meaning of this proverb, in terms of the destructive path of bribery, to *Proverbs* 14:12: "A road may seem right to a man, but in the end it is a road to death."

THE CLASSICIST:

Indeed. Now, to try to summarize what we've been saying about the Jewish Bible, there is no doubt that bribery
intended to subvert justice is uncompromisingly condemned.
Minor gift-giving, however, can be tolerated when such gifts
are an accepted norm to induce an official to act properly
in his or her formal capacity. The biblical eras were times of
gift-giving, often without sinister motivations. That's what I
take from my reading.

THE ECONOMIST:

I must say that I'm pleasantly surprised. I'm reassured that
biblical attitudes to gifts and bribery seem to accord largely
with my views, which are derived from economics.

THE PRIEST:

We shall need to discuss this in more detail later. I'm not convinced that the Bible backs up your economic arguments.
But I agree with my learned friend that the Old Testament
differentiates clearly between legitimate gifts and unacceptable bribes. Some gifts are simply gestures of goodwill rather
than bribes, especially in view of the asymmetrical information and power between those who hold positions of legal or
administrative authority and the general public.[54]

---

[54] The participants in the discussion do not explore the theme of
asymmetrical power relations in gift-giving in the Jewish Bible, but it has
been suggested that the Jewish Bible "seems to reflect a recognition of
the power differential between a poor person who gives a gift in order to
stave off injustice and the rich who uses his power to exploit the poor. The
powerful and the powerless are not judged by the same abstract absolute, but by the relationships and intentions of their situation" (Tawney,
1995, 165).

But, if you allow me, I'd now like to proceed to a discussion of the New Testament. As we've said, the New Testament builds on the Jewish biblical writings, and so it does not need to repeat in detail what the Old Testament has already made clear. So, in the New Testament, there are no extensive discussions of bribery: It is through some notable examples of bribes, and attempted bribes, that the ethical message is conveyed.

THE STUDENT:

It seems finally to be the time to introduce Judas Iscariot into our discussions.

THE PRIEST:

Yes, and more besides. The most striking example of bribery in the New Testament is, of course, the one that is central to Judas Iscariot's betrayal of Christ. The magnitude of the outcome is, of course, immeasurable, and this contrasts with the trivial sum offered to Judas. His bribe is only thirty pieces of silver,[55] far less than the enormous amounts of silver offered to Delilah to betray Samson.[56]

THE CLASSICIST:

Perhaps the thirty pieces of silver were symbolic. In *Exodus* they reflected the cost of compensating the death of a slave.[57]

---

[55] *Matthew* 26:15.

[56] See n. 38 above.

[57] Thirty shekels of silver was the blood price to be paid in the case of a servant or slave accidentally killed (*Exodus* 21:32), with all the allegorical allusions that this connection might have implied to the New Testament author. In addition, for women, the sum of thirty shekels of silver was related to the custom of pledging one's valuation in silver to the sanctuary (*Leviticus* 27:4).

THE PRIEST:

Perhaps. In any case, for our purposes, it's clear that the New Testament portrays Judas as a heinous bribe taker. His very name has become a byword for betrayal, and the thirty pieces of silver are the eternal symbol of a sinister bribe. He is the epitome of evil.[58]

THE CLASSICIST:

As you know, I'm no expert on the New Testament. But I'd like to probe this question of Judas a little further. There are some dark undercurrents to the Judas story, to put it mildly. But, first, I'm aware that there are differences among the biblical accounts of Judas, or at least some ambiguities. If this is correct, then what does it tell us about the meaning of this bribe and the role it played in Judas's motives?

THE PRIEST:

You're right: There *are* differences in the biblical Judas narratives. But, throughout the New Testament, the link between

---

[58] The Judas traditions are crystallized in the *Inferno* of Dante's *Divina Commedia*, which places Judas in the lowest circle of Hell, one of three sinners deemed sufficiently evil to be doomed to an eternity of being chewed in the mouths of a triple-headed Satan. Brioschi (2017, 13 and 54–55) reminds us that notorious Italian bribe takers of the thirteenth and fourteenth centuries (including Fra Gomita and Bonturo Dati) also found themselves in the sixth to ninth circles of Hell, and that, ironically, Dante himself was accused of similar crimes. Noonan (1984, 252) informs us that "if Canto 19 on simony is added, three and one-third, out of 30 cantos on the inhabitants of hell, are devoted to bribe-takers and their fate". This non-negligible proportion reflects the gravity of bribery in the Christian tradition. See ns. 73 and 137.

the bribe of silver coins and Judas's actions is clear. John tells us that Judas's betrayal of Jesus for money was, in part, a matter of character: He "was a thief; he kept the common purse and used to steal what was put in it".[59] His alleged financial misconduct while acting as treasurer to Christ and his disciples fits well with his acceptance of the history-changing bribe.

One thing I find interesting is that only one of the four Gospels, *Matthew*, tells us that Judas's life ends badly, with regret, repentance, and suicide. According to *Matthew*, Judas tried to return the thirty pieces of silver to the chief priests before hanging himself. The chief priests refused to accept the return of Judas's "blood money"[60] after which Judas threw the silver coins on the floor of the temple before going away to hang himself. The chief priests used the money to buy a field for the burial of foreigners.[61] So perhaps the thirty pieces of silver wasn't so trivial, after all, if it was sufficient to purchase land. And in the *Acts of the Apostles,*[62] there is a different, even more horrific, account of the end of Judas's life: He himself purchases a plot of land, on which, "falling headlong, he burst open in the middle and all his bowels gushed out".[63] This gruesome disembowelment seemed fitting for the hideous nature of Judas's behavior. But in all the New Testament accounts, there is a common theme: Judas's behavior is unequivocally evil, and his betrayal of Jesus is

---

[59] *John* 12:6.
[60] The expression "blood money" refers to money used in the killing of an innocent person.
[61] *Matthew* 27:3–10.
[62] Generally attributed to the author of the *Gospel of Luke*.
[63] *Acts* 1:18.

linked inextricably to the bribe of thirty pieces of silver.[64] It made him beyond redemption.[65]

THE CLASSICIST:

Thank you for this explanation. And I believe there are more differences throughout the New Testament in the way the Judas narrative is handled.

THE PRIEST:

Yes. There are quite a few differences, in terms of his actions and motives. Some of these differences might be tied to the chronology of the writing of the individual books of the New Testament, which I think, for our present purposes, is too big a subject to enter into with a lot of detail, but we can nonetheless take at least a glance at it. In the two earliest Gospels, *Mark* and *Matthew*, Jesus says that "it would have been better for that one [Judas] not to have been born".[66] In the two later Gospels, *Luke* and *John,* we're told that Satan "entered into"[67] Judas. *John* also tells us that "the Devil had already put it into the heart of Judas son of Simon Iscariot to betray [Jesus]".[68] This shows that Judas's portrayal becomes

---

[64] It is interesting to note that the noncanonical, second century Gnostic *Gospel of Judas* (published in the modern public domain only in the early twenty-first century) praised Judas for his role in triggering humanity's salvation and exalted Judas as the best of the disciples, yet it still retained a reference to his bribe-taking. The final sentence of the *Gospel of Judas* states the following: "And Judas received money and handed him [Jesus] over to them" (Kasser and Wurst, 2006, 235). Therefore, even a document that seems to claim that Judas was the disciple who was closest to Jesus, and with whom Jesus collaborated to set in motion the events that were to redeem mankind, does not dispense with the notorious bribe in its narrative.

[65] See n. 58 for the treatment Dante gives to Judas in his vision of Hell.

[66] *Mark* 14:21, *Matthew* 26:24.

[67] *Luke* 22:3, *John* 13:27.

[68] *John* 13:2.

progressively more satanic from *Mark* to *John*, in accordance with the currently presumed chronology of the authorship of the Gospels.[69]

THE CLASSICIST:

There's something else in the New Testament account of Judas that troubles me. It's beyond doubt that Judas has been a lightning rod for anti-Semitism. Traditionally, for anti-Semites, Judas became the personification of the Jews, and he has been central to Christian accusations of Jewish deicide.[70]

THE PRIEST:

Alas, you are of course correct. It's a terrible legacy of the Judas tradition.

THE ECONOMIST:

Shall we try to proceed to pull together the biblical themes before we move on to other areas of discussion?

THE PRIEST:

No, no, no. I've only discussed the Judas bribe! The New Testament mentions bribery elsewhere, with important

---

[69] These comments assume a chronological sequence of *Mark*, *Matthew*, *Luke*, and *John* in the dating of the canonical Gospels. Indeed, this sequence has scholarly support—see, for example, Meyer (2007, 27).

[70] Judas is the Greek version of Judah, one of Jacob's twelve sons and patriarch of the eponymous tribe, which gave its name to the area around Jerusalem. Judas appears to have been a popular Jewish name at the time of the events in the New Testament (as was its female equivalent, Judith). See Gathercole (2007, 25 and 158). For examples of the role of the Judas traditions in the Holocaust, see Desbois (2018, 87–90).

ramifications. There are not too many of these references, but they're crucial to our discussion.

THE STUDENT:

Let's hear them.

THE PRIEST:

In *Matthew*, alone among the Gospels, it's recounted that the Roman soldiers charged with guarding Jesus's tomb were bribed with a "large sum of money" to lie about the disappearance of Jesus's body in order to stifle stories of the resurrection.[71] This is a clear example of the corrupting influence of bribery, with the intention of spreading untruths.

There are also two episodes in the *Acts of the Apostles* in which bribes are offered but rejected. First, Simon the Magician tries to bribe the apostles Peter and John with money in exchange for the ability to bestow the power of the Holy Spirit. Peter replies: "May your silver perish with you because you thought you could obtain God's gift with money!"[72] In this way, we learn that the apostles, by resisting the bribe, maintain their integrity.[73] Second, Marcus Antonius Felix, the Roman procurator of Judea, kept Saint Paul in prison under the guise of protective custody. Felix hoped to receive a bribe to end Saint Paul's unjust incarceration, but the bribe never materialized: Saint Paul refused to pay it.[74] These narratives contain very important denunciations of

---

[71] *Matthew* 28:12–15.

[72] *Acts* 8:20.

[73] The episode of Simon the Magician gave rise to the term "simony", the corrupt practice of selling ecclesiastical offices and spiritual privileges. Noonan (1984, 59) describes Simon as "a double, a negative image of [Simon] Peter the Rock, the leader of the Apostles". See also ns. 58 and 137 and the discussion of simony in Section Four.

[74] *Acts* 24:26.

bribery's inherently corrupting nature, and they highlight the importance of resisting the temptations of bribery.

THE CLASSICIST:

The message conveyed by these incidents seems clear: Bribery is wrong.

THE PRIEST:

To wrap up our discussions of the New Testament, we may consider an oblique or implied reference by Christ to bribery. When challenged over the religious justification of paying taxes to the Roman emperor, the response is well known: "Give...to Caesar the things that are Caesar's, and to God the things that are God's."[75] This statement is widely interpreted as a teaching for the Christian to reconcile divine and secular law[76] and also as a basis for the future separation of church and state. However, we mustn't forget that, in New Testament times, paying taxes invariably involved paying the bribes and extorted amounts bundled up with the taxes. Tax collectors were notorious for inflating tax payments and skimming off the excess.[77] I therefore have to raise a tricky issue: Could Christ be saying that it's acceptable to pay bribes if they are unavoidable in daily life and bundled up with legitimate legal obligations, provided that one's intention is not to subvert

---

[75] *Matthew* 22:21.

[76] See also *Romans* 13:1 on the topic of obedience to worldly authorities.

[77] The priest may also have mentioned John the Baptist's comments on bribery and extortion: "Even tax collectors came to be baptized, and they asked him, 'Teacher, what should we do?' He said to them, 'Collect no more than the amount prescribed for you.' Soldiers also asked him, 'And we, what should we do?' He [John the Baptist] said to them, 'Do not extort money from anyone by threats or false accusations, and be satisfied with your wages'." (*Luke* 3:12–14)

justice? I think this may well be the case, on the condition that the secular authorities are deserving of obedience. This would tie in with the Old Testament's distinguishing between legitimate gift-giving and justice-subverting bribery.

THE CLASSICIST:

I think this is a significant point. We saw that the Jewish Bible seems to differentiate gifts on the basis of their nature and their consequences—those that subvert justice are bribes, while those that are minor or unavoidable in social interactions are permissible gifts. The specific instances of bribe takers in the New Testament narratives, like Judas and the soldiers keeping watch over the tomb, and the unsuccessful solicitation of bribes from Peter and Paul, all clearly show that a bribe is motivated by power and greed and that it subverts justice. But the example you gave of paying taxes that are likely to be bundled up with bribes shows us, I think, that the Christian Bible does leave some space for the types of unavoidable gift-giving that do not violate justice.

THE PRIEST:

Yes. And, in addition, the generosity of unselfish gift-giving is also emphasized. In *Matthew*, Christ says to his followers: "You have received without payment; give without payment."[78] To me, Christ's instruction to give freely refers to matters beyond simple, mundane gift-giving—this type of giving is the dispensation of God's gifts, from healing the sick to raising the dead, revealing the power of Christ in the widest sense.

---

[78] *Matthew* 10:8.

THE ECONOMIST:

And look at the gifts given to the newly born Jesus by the mysterious wise men:[79] These were surely pure gifts, apparently given without any thought of a *quid pro quo*.

THE PRIEST:

One more thing: We heard earlier an example of the treatment of bribery in the Jewish Oral Law.[80] It's important to remember that the development of Christianity also did not end with the Bible: There is a rich tradition of Christian theological development, through the Fathers and Doctors of the Church and, indeed, to the present day. I'd like to draw attention to a very relevant aspect of Church tradition—that of excessive scrupulosity.[81]

THE STUDENT:

There we go again. You talk nonchalantly about the "Fathers" of the Church: It shows that you are dealing with a traditional, patriarchal system that has a questionable relevance to today's concerns.

THE ECONOMIST:

Look, there'll be plenty of time to explore the point of view of the *soixante-huitards*[82] later. I want to hear a little more about what the Church tradition has to say on this topic.

---

[79] *Matthew* 2:11.

[80] See n. 43.

[81] A translation of the Latin *scruples*, which indicates a pathological and unwarranted fear of committing sin. The problem of a fanatical and obsessive attachment to religious devotion in medieval times is reflected in modern, secular psychiatric disorders of obsessive-compulsive behavior.

[82] See n. 11.

THE PRIEST:

My point is that the Church identified scrupulosity as a sin, and even as the work of the Devil. A fanatical obsession with committing sin doesn't allow a person to function properly. One can become ethically paralyzed by a fear of sinning. There has to be discernment between grave sins and lesser sins and between sins and non-sins. The implication for bribery, I would say, is that one should not, according to Christian tradition, fret too much over minor gifts. If a gift is socially expected and is not intended to subvert justice, then, to put it simply, don't beat yourself up over it. Excessive moral absolutism is the enemy of true morality because it distorts ethical judgement and paralyzes action.

THE ECONOMIST:

I'm very pleasantly surprised that what you are saying accords reasonably well with my economic-based arguments. We should make space for minor bribes that may have positive outcomes.

THE PRIEST:

Within the parameters of the discussion we've had so far, you may be correct. But we haven't discussed yet in detail your economic arguments.

THE STUDENT:

And let's not forget that, right now, we're discussing religious texts of limited relevance to many people today. What you're saying is of largely antiquarian interest. But we're not archaeologists. We're here to discuss the world as it is today.

THE CLASSICIST:

With all due respect, please allow me to disagree with you. As we unfold our discussions, you may find a logical and consistent basis for the traditional ethics of gift-giving.

THE STUDENT:

Be that as it may, I have a final question on the religious topics we've been subjected to. Please understand that I'm not being intentionally mischievous, but I have to ask this question: Isn't prayer to God a form of bribery?

THE PRIEST:

(Laughs). That's a very good question. I think we should take care not to interpret as bribery too many episodes in the Bible. For example, in the Garden of Eden, some say that the snake's temptation of Eve with the apple was a bribe. Of course, this is incorrect: Eve is disobedient, but she's not involved in bribery.[83] So we should be careful.

Specifically, in the relations between God and humans, there is certainly a kind of reciprocity involved. Here we go back to the distinction between gifts and bribes: God asks us for the former but not, of course, for the latter. We started our discussion of bribery in the Bible by quoting the condemnation of bribery from *Exodus*.[84] Well, later in the same chapter of *Exodus*, God says: "None shall appear before me empty-handed."[85] This means that God expects gifts, in the

---

[83] *Genesis* 3:1–7. See Noonan (1984, 22): "...the serpent does not offer the apple, he merely points out the beneficial consequences of eating... Eve's sin is not bribetaking but disobedience."

[84] See n. 28.

[85] *Exodus* 23:15.

form of sacrificial offerings in those days and today in the form of prayer.

THE STUDENT:

Are we to understand that the bigger the believer's gifts or the more time spent in prayer, the greater the favors God dispenses? Isn't this simply a way of favoring the rich and the powerful who can afford the most impressive gifts or who have the most leisure time for prayer?

THE CLASSICIST:

Not at all. The first gifts given to God in the Bible are those brought by Cain and Abel. And let's look at what happens: It's interesting that God accepts Abel's gift but not Cain's.[86] There's some theological dispute as to the basis for God's rejection of Cain's offering, but it seems to me to boil down to the view that the donor has to be worthy. It's not really about the gift itself; instead, it has everything to do with the intentions and behavior of the donor.[87] The whole system of tithes and animal sacrifices and prayers that developed from this origin has, of course, been subjected to abuse at times. But that has been a perversion of the intention: It doesn't affect the underlying truth about gifts and God in the Bible. And, as we'll see in due course in our discussions of the Greeks, Plato also pointed out that one of the greatest impieties is the notion that the gods can be bribed.[88]

---

[86] *Genesis* 4:3–7.

[87] "Abel seems to have demonstrated a quality of heart and mind that Cain did not possess. Cain's purpose was noble, but his act was not ungrudging and openhearted. Thus the narrative conveys the fundamental principle of Judaism that the act of worship must be informed by genuine devotion of the heart." (Sarna, 1991, 32–33).

[88] See n. 115.

THE PRIEST:

Let me add the observation that God's acceptance of gifts is His way of achieving a compromise between the mundane world of humanity and the spiritual substance of divine order. What are perceived as *quid pro quo* reciprocities between humanity and God have nothing to do with crude magic or favoritism towards the powerful. It's simply an expression of the constitution of human existence in divine law.

THE CLASSICIST:

Exactly. Prayer and other gifts to God are a bridge between the immanence of our world and the transcendence of God. And now, I think it's time we embarked on a brief look at the ancient Greeks and at their attitudes to bribery. Then we can pull these strands together, blending Jerusalem with Athens, as I like to say. At that point, we'll be in a position to assess the extent to which we, in the contemporary world, are bound by our antique heritage. Or perhaps we'll find that we've been uprooted from our heritage, and we've ended up in our own *bateau ivre*,[89] cast on a sea of doubt and uncertainty.

THE PRIEST:

You are obviously best placed to kick off this part of our analysis.

THE ECONOMIST:

But, if you allow me, before we proceed, I'd like to summarize what we've heard up to this point. I've been taking

---

[89] "Drunken boat". A reference to the Arthur Rimbaud (1854–1891) poem of 1871, in which the poet describes a symbolic boat journey of disorder and disaster.

notes, and I've been struck by something I wasn't expecting. I expected biblical morality to be purely of a duty-bound persuasion, as one might expect from divine commands, but, it seems to me, there are also elements of consequentialism in what we've heard.[90] The Bible encourages judgment, and not merely blind obedience.

THE PRIEST:

Of course. The Bible isn't simply a list of rules. It invites thought and reflection, and reasoning. Jews and Christians don't simply look up a rule. They have to assess the evidence and decide when a gift runs the risk of becoming a bribe.

THE ECONOMIST:

I hadn't anticipated the extent of this. When I say there are elements of consequentialism, I'm referring to matters like the Old Testament's differentiation between gifts as a social expectation and bribes that subvert justice. Judgment is clearly needed to interpret these matters, so that we can assess the consequences of a gift. Also, what has been suggested about the implications of paying Caesar his due, even if this is well known to include unavoidable bribes, really opened my eyes. If this is understood in the context of

---

[90] The economist draws attention to contrasting ethical approaches to be featured throughout the subsequent discussions. He contrasts, on one side, divine command and secular deontological or duty-based ethics (for example, Kantian ethics) in which an act's consequences are secondary (though not entirely unimportant) to its intrinsic wrongness, with, on the other side, consequentialist ethics in which the rightness or wrongness of an act depends mainly on its consequences. The economist relies on utilitarian ethics (expounded in Section Five) which are a form of consequentialist ethics. In practice, it is not always easy to differentiate between the two approaches. Moral pluralists combine the two by considering consequences as important, but not exclusively so.

scrupulosity,[91] it's clear that the Bible doesn't just tell us what to do. It seems to urge us to reflect on the consequences of our actions. And there seem to be some connections between the biblical view and the case I can make for the acceptability of some categories of small bribes that resemble gifts. Anyway, we're at an early stage of our discussions, so let's proceed with a consideration of the Greek approach to bribery.

_____

[91] See n. 81.

Chapter Three
Bribery and the Greeks

THE CLASSICIST:

I have to admit that it's with a certain trepidation that I embark on this stage of our investigation. The reason? The subject matter is so immense. So I've decided to restrict myself largely to the thought of Plato and Socrates.

THE PRIEST:

What? No Aristotle?

THE CLASSICIST:

To me, it seems that Aristotle presented some topics that are very relevant to the theme of our discussions, and I'll refer to them as necessary. But he won't be the focus of my discussions. The core of what I have to say can, I believe, be found in the thought of Plato and Socrates.

THE STUDENT:

My understanding is that Socrates never wrote anything down, or anything he did write hasn't survived. So how can you differentiate between Socrates and his student, Plato?

THE CLASSICIST:

That's a big and important topic: The borderline at which Socratic teaching ends and Platonic innovation begins is problematic. For our purposes, I'd merely point out that we have independent evidence of Socrates's teachings beyond what we learn from Plato.[92] It might be possible, to a degree, to reconstruct Socratic thought as distinct from Plato's. But it's a task fraught with difficulties. So, bearing in mind that the overlap between Socrates and Plato is often unclear, let's get started.

THE PRIEST:

I, for one, am anxious to hear what you're going to say.

THE CLASSICIST:

Let me start with an analogy. Just as we found that the Bible's views on bribery have to be interpreted in the context of its wider moral message, in the Ten Commandments and the Sermon on the Mount and so on, similarly in Plato we must consider the wider moral framework in which bribery is considered. There are not very many references to bribery in Plato's writings, but what is written about bribery must be understood in the context of Platonic ethics. And, therefore, it seems to me we must start with the four cardinal virtues.[93]

---

[92] The most extensive, surviving record of Socrates's thoughts and discussions outside the Platonic corpus was recorded by Xenophon (c. 430–354 BCE).

[93] The term *arete* (ἀρετή) has been translated as "virtue" in this text. An alternative translation could have been "moral excellence", in the sense of a fulfillment of moral potential.

THE STUDENT:

Which are?

THE CLASSICIST:

Justice, courage, moderation, and wisdom.[94] These terms carry a lot of baggage, but they don't lose too much in the translations I've given, at least for our purposes today. We all have a fair idea of what we mean when we talk of justice, courage, and moderation. The notion of wisdom is a little trickier. Sometimes this virtue is referred to as prudence or sound judgment, but I prefer to say wisdom. What's intended here is a kind of intelligent approach to life, founded on sensible behavior that is appropriate to the circumstances.

Now, let's note that these four virtues shouldn't be seen in the same light as the Ten Commandments. The Greek virtues were not so much rules to be followed as aspects of one's character. Putting this another way, the virtues were not a list of duties but more like states of being or dispositions that drive one's behavior.

THE ECONOMIST:

If the Greeks didn't look on the virtues as a list of rules, thinking of them more along the lines of character traits, did they consider it necessary to exhibit all four cardinal virtues or just

---

[94] In this text *dikaiosyne* (δικαιοσύνη) has been translated as "justice", *andreia* (ἀνδρεία) as "courage", *sophrosyne* (σωφροσύνη) as "moderation", and *phronesis* (φρόνησις) as "wisdom". One of the more challenging of these terms for translators is φρόνησῖς: It refers to a type of wisdom or intelligence that is relevant to practical action, implying both good judgment and excellence of character and habits. References to the cardinal virtues are widespread in Plato's writings. Notable examples include *Republic* 427e and *Alcibiades* I 121e–122a (but the authorship of the latter dialogue is disputed).

one or more of them? And, if so, did the virtues carry different weights? In other words, was there a hierarchy of value
between the virtues?

THE CLASSICIST:

You're posing very searching questions. The relationships
between the virtues were not definitively established and
have been the subject of much debate. Indeed, Socrates or
Plato, or perhaps Plato's Socrates, did at times entertain the
notion that the four virtues were a unity. Perhaps this meant
they were identical in the sense that the individual pieces of
a gold nugget that has been shattered into smaller fragments
are identical. Alternatively, and this to me seems more likely,
the virtues were distinct yet interrelated parts of a whole, in
the way that the mouth, nose, ears, and eyes are part of a
face.[95] The matter wasn't settled. But I'd say that, in general, a
fully virtuous person would need to display all the four virtues.

THE STUDENT:

But couldn't a person be, let's say, courageous and yet simul-
taneously unwise? Like a soldier running recklessly into battle, without thought for his or her safety?

THE CLASSICIST:

Absolutely. This is a fascinating topic so, before we move
on, let's pause to explore the unity of the virtues. If the four
virtues can be separated, does this mean that some virtues

---

[95] The theme of the unity of the virtues, expressed in the analogies of
the human face and the nugget of gold, are found in *Protagoras* 329d–e.
In *Laws* 963c–e, the Athenian Stranger raises the question of the unity of
the virtues, but the matter is unresolved. The Xenophontic Socrates also
discusses the distinct nature of the virtues and leaves the extent of the
unity of the virtues somewhat unclear (Xenophon, *Memorabilia* III.9.4–6
and IV.6.1–11).

might be undesirable in the context of the absence of other virtues? It would appear to be the case from the example you just gave. If a soldier recklessly enters battle without careful consideration of how to fight, he may put his own life, as well as the other soldiers' lives, in peril. So courage surely needs to be tempered by wisdom and perhaps moderation if it is to be effective. So there is a strong case to be made that the virtues are to be understood together, supporting each other.

THE PRIEST:

I'd go further. I'd say that a single virtue might serve good or evil ends. Take, for example, a brave soldier who fights for an evil cause, like National Socialism.

THE ECONOMIST:

Good point. An individual Nazi soldier may have been brave and fearless, but his courage cannot have been virtuous because he was fighting for an evil cause. Courage must surely be matched with justice and the other virtues.

THE CLASSICIST:

Exactly. And when it comes to bribery, we may say that the principal virtue that concerns us is justice, as we saw in the Bible. If bribery subverts justice, then inevitably the virtue of justice is violated. But the other virtues may also be relevant to bribery. For example, it may take courage to resist a bribe if there is social or economic pressure to accept it. So we can add courage to justice.

THE STUDENT:

Remind me again of your four virtues.

THE CLASSICIST:

They are justice, courage, moderation, and wisdom. But they are hardly my virtues. They were established in the classical world.

THE STUDENT:

Based on the framework you're presenting, isn't moderation also important in the context of bribery?

THE ECONOMIST:

It must be, in the sense that one should moderate one's appetites. If a person can conquer his or her greed, making him or her resistant to the temptations of bribery, then the virtue of moderation is undoubtedly important.

THE PRIEST:

And wisdom is significant, too. I suppose that having a wise and commonsense approach to life allows one to weigh the costs and benefits, or the rightness and wrongness, of certain courses of action.

THE CLASSICIST:

You're all correct. Refusing a bribe might involve a combination of courage, wisdom, and a moderation of one's greed in order to achieve justice. All the points you've made are valid. But for the purposes of our discussion, I wish to focus on justice as the main virtue that is under attack, so to speak, from bribery. We saw, when discussing the Bible, that the biblical treatment of bribery focuses on bribery's subversion of justice. I propose we therefore discuss the classical virtues with a focus on justice, although not forgetting entirely the other virtues.

THE ECONOMIST:

If that will make your handling of this topic more manageable, then I don't see how we can disagree.

THE CLASSICIST:

Then, if there's no objection, please allow me to continue as follows. It seems to me that Plato, in his writings, is fighting the corruption he sees around himself in an ethically diseased society. The character of Socrates is a paradigm of good ethical behavior, and Plato presents Socrates as the opposite of the corrupt society in which he lives.

The corruption in ancient Athens undermines that city's justice, and bribery is one of the elements of this corruption. Socrates, of course, was free from the city's corruption, and especially free from bribery. For example, Socrates engaged in educational discussions with his followers, yet he never charged fees for his services. He seems to have had no real appetite for money and so, we might say, he exhibited the virtue of moderation.[96] It's not just money with which he was moderate: He also restrained his sexual appetites and led a simple life.[97]

---

[96] On Socrates's unwillingness to charge his discussion partners, see, for example, *Euthyphro* 3d-e. In contrast to Socrates's avoidance of fee-charging, the famous teachers of rhetoric of Plato's day were reported to charge substantial fees for their instruction (*Alcibiades* I 119a). Xenophon also provides evidence for Socrates's noncharging of fees in *Memorabilia* I.ii.5–8 and I.ii.60. See also Xenophon's evidence in Socrates's *Defence to the Jury* that Socrates's incorruptibility rested, in large part, on his not accepting gifts and money for his discussions: "Who is there in your knowledge that is less a slave to his bodily appetites than I am? Who in the world more free,—for I accept neither gifts nor pay from any one?" And "while other men get their delicacies in the markets and pay a high price for them, I devise more pleasurable ones from the resources of my soul, with no expenditure of money" (Loeb edition, 637–663).

[97] On Socrates's sexual restraint, see Alcibiades's speech in *Symposium* 215a–219e.

THE STUDENT:

A superman, we might say.

THE CLASSICIST:

An exemplary individual is my estimation of Socrates. His ability to moderate his behavior is central to our theme. It is difficult to bribe someone who won't accept even legitimate fees. And because he succeeded in holding his appetites in check, it is almost impossible, in my view, to see how he could be bribed. By using his reason to moderate his appetites, he was immune to bribery.

THE ECONOMIST:

But was Socrates's character ever put to the test with a real attempt at bribery?

THE CLASSICIST:

Yes, of course. As you undoubtedly know, Socrates was the victim of a judicial murder. Fundamentally, in my view, he was killed because of his tendency to speak truth to power and to challenge the received ideas of his day. When, at the age of seventy, Socrates was languishing in prison for several weeks following his trial, awaiting his execution, his friend Crito suggested bribing the jailers so that Socrates could escape to a life in exile. Naturally, Socrates declined the offer and informed Crito that his understanding of justice and loyalty to Athens required him to pay the ultimate price.[98] Essentially, Socrates refused to engage in one type

---

[98] Crito's offer is in *Crito* 44a–46a, and Socrates's justification of his acceptance of his death sentence is set out in both *Crito* and *Phaedo*, passim.

of injustice, bribery, to counter another injustice, his unfair execution.[99]

THE PRIEST:

Well, I'd say that Socrates's refusal to escape his execution through bribery is a resounding example of a principled stance against bribery. The message couldn't be clearer, especially as his very life was at stake.

THE CLASSICIST:

When you consider that Socrates was unjustly convicted, or at least that his sentence was too extreme, then you're one hundred per cent correct. It's hard to think of a clearer condemnation of bribery as an act that undermines injustice.

THE ECONOMIST:

Your conclusion is, indeed, difficult to refute.

THE CLASSICIST:

But let's go a little deeper into the topic of justice in Plato. In the *Republic*, there's a profound reflection on...

THE STUDENT:

The *Republic*? Seriously? You're going to support your arguments with that fascistic text? I can't think of a worse example of the subversion of justice.

---

[99] There is some scholarly difference of opinion as to whether Socrates should have been found guilty or innocent of the charges of impiety and corrupting the youth of Athens, as reported by Plato. See Brickhouse and Smith (2002).

THE ECONOMIST:

I admit to sharing some concerns about the *Republic*. We all know that the *Republic* is a blueprint for a totalitarian state. It advocates eugenics and extreme collectivization. It's difficult to see how you can use it as a paradigm of justice.[100]

THE CLASSICIST:

You raise an important concern but, in my opinion, it's not a valid objection. It's undoubtedly true that the *Republic* sets out a utopian state that has aspects we are bound to find objectionable. But, however much I'd like to discuss this topic, I fear that if we digress too far, then we'll go astray.

THE ECONOMIST:

Without going into too much depth, I think you need to say something more to set our minds at ease regarding the *Republic*, especially if you are going to refer to the *Republic* to support your arguments concerning the virtue of justice.

THE CLASSICIST:

Alright. Let me set out my opinions on this matter. Plato chose to express his ideas through dialogues rather than through theses or lecture notes, in the manner of Aristotle. And Plato's dialogues might be understood as mixtures of recollections of Socrates's discussions and dramatizations of Plato's own thoughts. The dialogues are rich with analogies with the wider Greek culture of the day, and they contain an enormous range of viewpoints, often conflicting and irreconcilable.

---

[100] The student and the economist seem to be referring to a tradition of viewing the *Republic* as a literal blueprint for an unjust, authoritarian state. See Popper (1945).

And let's not forget that Plato himself never appears in his dialogues, so we cannot be sure what Plato's views really are. It's therefore notoriously difficult to try to distil a Platonic dogma from his writings. That's one reason why Plato's successors in his Academy swung between widely differing and often incompatible interpretations of the Platonic tradition. There was no fixed dogma of Plato's to be followed.[101]

THE STUDENT:

Plato gives us Socrates in most of his dialogues. Socrates was his virtuous superman, in a manner of speaking, so can't we broadly assume that Socrates speaks for Plato?

THE CLASSICIST:

Not necessarily. The borderline between Socratic thought and Platonic thought is very difficult to establish, as I hinted earlier. And Socrates was known for his irony, so it's not at all clear when Socrates may or may not be saying what he thinks. Socrates aims to elicit responses from his discussion partners, and he seems to use a range of tactics for this. Sometimes, as I just mentioned, he might be saying the opposite of what he thinks, or he may even, on occasion, lead a discussion in a deliberately false direction for the educative purposes of the dialogue.

So, to come back to the *Republic* and to try not to digress too far, let's concede that the communistic, authoritarian, utopian city-state of Callipolis[102] sacrifices many freedoms, including private property. But is this really what Socrates or Plato advocated? Personally, I don't take the *Republic*

---

[101] See, for example, Dillon (2003) and Tarán (1981) on the evolution of interpretations of Plato's legacy in his Academy following his death.

[102] Καλλίπολις—the beautiful city—is rendered either as Callipolis or Kallipolis in English translations.

seriously as a political blueprint for a state: It's more what a state would look like if it were totally structured towards the inculcation of virtue. I'm inclined to the view that Plato was depicting the unacceptable sacrifices of individual freedom that would have to be made to search for a rigidly perfect political dispensation, and Plato wanted instead to warn of the risks we might run in a search for perfection. In other words, he may be treating Callipolis as an allegory of the soul, and at the same time showing us the dangers inherent in following logic to its utopian conclusions.

THE PRIEST:

I see here a connection with what I said earlier about scrupulosity[103] in the Church tradition, in terms of the importance of maintaining a balanced and nonfanatical approach to moral matters.

THE STUDENT:

Hold on, please! Would you really have us believe that Plato's *Republic* conveys the opposite of what a plain reading would indicate?

THE ECONOMIST:

Certainly a plain reading would suggest that it's a blueprint for—or even an inspiration for—a fascist state.

THE CLASSICIST:

I maintain that Plato wasn't a fanatical collectivist. Look, for example, at the far more mellow city of Magnesia portrayed in the *Laws*, written towards the end of Plato's life. Magnesia is

[103] See n. 81.

not a utopian city nor an authoritarian one. It's governed not by autocratic philosopher-kings but by impartial law, and it's far closer to what we would recognize as a reasonable political dispensation.

THE STUDENT:

Are you being serious?

THE CLASSICIST:

Yes, I'm being totally serious. But I think that we're going to end up in very deep waters if we pursue this digression much further. Interpreting Plato is extremely difficult. Some people take a literal reading. Others tend to allegorize Plato. Some say that Plato had unwritten or esoteric doctrines that supplemented or even underpinned his written dialogues.[104] So, if you'll permit me, I'd like briefly to present my arguments relating to justice in the *Republic*, and we'll see if they make sense.

THE PRIEST:

I think you should proceed. Otherwise, our discussion will end up going around in circles.

---

[104] A reference to Plato's alleged "unwritten doctrines" (*agrapha dogmata*, ἄγραφα δόγματα) channeled through oral transmission and recorded patchily in various sources (Nikulin, 2012). The unwritten doctrines approach is principally associated, in the modern era, with the German *Tübinger Platonschule* centered on the University of Tübingen. For example, Szlezák (1999, 79) has put the case that Plato's "writing remains basically reliant on oral supplementation by 'things of greater value'". A closely related school of thought has developed in Italy, influenced by Giovanni Reale (1931–2014): The resulting German/Italian tradition is sometimes referred to as the *Scuola di Tubinga-Milano*, and Reale (2008) provides an overview of its teachings. The existence, significance, and interpretation of Plato's inner-Academy "things of greater value" (*timiotera*, τιμιότερα), mentioned in *Phaedrus* 278d, are disputed.

THE STUDENT:

Very well. Let's go on.

THE CLASSICIST:

In the opening line of the *Republic*, we're told that Socrates "went down" from Athens to the nearby port town of Piraeus. The significance of this opening line is often overlooked. It tends to be assumed to be little more than the adding of some local color to the setting. But for me it has immense meaning.

THE ECONOMIST:

In what way?

THE CLASSICIST:

The notion of "going down" reflects not just the journey from Athens to Piraeus but also a journey into the darkness of the Platonic Cave[105] and the subsequent escape from shadowy illusions to the clarity of sunlit truth. It may also echo Homer's portrayal of Odysseus's account to Penelope of his descent to Hades[106] to seek advice on how to make his way home. Just as Odysseus subsequently left the cave-like darkness of Hades to continue his arduous journey homeward, and just as the prisoner escaped Plato's dark cave for the sunlight of truth, so Socrates decided to leave the mediocrity and lack of wisdom of his discussion partners in Piraeus and return to Athens. What we're dealing with is an intellectual journey: a search for truth.

---

[105] *Republic* 514a–517c.

[106] *Odyssey* 23:251–253. See the comments of Voegelin (2000, 106–116) on this analogy.

THE STUDENT:

Aren't we still getting bogged down in trivial matters?

THE CLASSICIST:

Then let's go right to the heart of the matter. In Plato's *Republic*, the three virtues of wisdom, courage, and moderation are distributed between three groups of citizens in the city-state of Callipolis. The ruling class is taught about the ultimate Good, for which they need wisdom. The military class needs to possess courage, obviously, and moderation is primarily associated with the third class, the working class of farmers and producers. Thus, the city is wise as a whole because of its wise rulers, brave as a whole because of its brave soldiers, and moderate as a whole because of its workers. The three virtues are in harmony.

THE ECONOMIST:

And the fourth virtue, justice?

THE CLASSICIST:

Justice governs the proper relationship between itself and the other three virtues.

THE STUDENT:

I'm lost. What's your point?

THE CLASSICIST:

What I'm trying to convey is that Plato, in the *Republic*, seems to be saying that not all classes of citizens may individually display each virtue,[107] but collectively the cardinal virtues are present in the city.[108] Therefore, some virtues alone may not need to be prominent at the level of the individual person, or group of people, provided that they can be found elsewhere in the city. Each person displays the virtue appropriate to his or her social role in the wider society, and an overall unity and harmony are achieved from the various components. Justice is the result.

THE STUDENT:

No, I'm still lost. I don't see what brave soldiers and moderate workers have to do with bribery.

THE CLASSICIST:

Alright. I'll put things another way. The *Republic* suggests to us that, in the ideal political arrangement, wise leadership is provided by the rulers, freedom is protected by the courage of the soldiers, and food and material goods are secured by the moderate disposition of the workers. In this tripartite social and political structure, a division of labor and of responsibilities leads to efficiency and also, Plato suggests, to justice.

---

[107] This theme appears elsewhere in Plato's writings. For example, Protagoras suggests that an individual person might display some of the virtues but not the others: "...many are courageous but unjust, and many again are just but not wise" (*Protagoras* 329e).

[108] See also the *Statesman*, in which the Visitor suggests to the young Socrates that moderation and courage may be present together in only a few individuals, as most people exhibit one or other of these virtues, and that the wise ruler will try to reconcile the two types of individual by "the weaving together, with regular intertwining, of the dispositions of brave and moderate people" (311b-c).

THE PRIEST:

I think I understand what you're saying. Justice results from the implementation of the other three cardinal virtues.

THE CLASSICIST:

Exactly. And the next step is hugely important. Socrates draws a parallel in the *Republic* between justice in the three social classes of Callipolis and justice in the individual, who is composed of a tripartite soul. Just as Socrates identifies justice as a virtue derived from the other three virtues in the political state, he suggests that justice exists in the human soul as a result of the harmonious coexistence of the same three virtues in the individual's soul.

To summarize, the conception of the state in the *Republic* separates people into three categories: rulers, soldiers, and producers. If the rulers, through wisdom, create just laws, and the soldiers courageously defend the city and its laws, and the workers obey the authorities, with moderate and productive ways of living, then the society as a whole will be just. By analogy, within the individual soul, if reason represents wisdom, which rules the spirited aspects of one's character (manifested in anger, indignation, and, importantly for our discussion, courage) and which moderates the appetite for physical desires, then the individual person will be just.[109] The presence of the three other virtues leads to justice at the level of the political unit and the individual person.

You're all silent. Was I clear enough?

---

[109] The tripartite division of the soul also appears in *Phaedrus* 246a–254e: Plato uses the allegory of reason as a charioteer who handles two horses, one of whom is passionate and impatient, the other calm, to symbolize the role of reason in self-control.

THE ECONOMIST:

I think I've grasped the essence of what you've been saying about the tripartite division of the political state and the individual's soul. The political community is man written large. Or perhaps man is the political community on a smaller scale.

THE CLASSICIST:

Precisely. My personal view is that Plato went to the trouble of showing us justice in the city first because it is far more visible than justice in the soul. But, ultimately, they're closely related.

THE STUDENT:

I don't like use of the word "soul" in this discussion.

THE CLASSICIST:

We can substitute "soul" with "personality", "consciousness" or "character" to make it less metaphysical and more down-to-earth. Now, perhaps, you can see why I felt a sense of trepidation in the face of the magnitude of this topic. We could hold an entire discussion solely about the tripartite division of the city and the soul. But let me try to cut even deeper through the details to the core of my argument on bribery.

For Plato, moral confusion was the cause of political and personal disorder. In the *Republic*, Plato's Socrates embarks on a project in which he seeks to establish an ethical basis for governing both a political state and an individual person. The three elements of the state and the individual's soul, or personality, reflect the three cardinal virtues other than justice, and the harmonious combination of the three virtues leads to the implementation of justice. As I indicated just now, the three social classes in Callipolis are the rulers, the soldiers, and the producers, and these are analogous to reason, spirit, and appetite in the soul. Respectively, therefore, the individual's reason, spirit, and appetite relate to the virtues of wisdom, courage, and moderation.

The *Republic* therefore sets out a vision of humans at peace with themselves and with others, in accordance with an internal harmony that leads to justice. This is not necessarily based on any postmortem rewards for good conduct in an afterlife (though it may be), but rather it's understood as being inherent in our worldly arrangements. As Socrates himself says: "[I]n establishing our [utopian] city, we aren't aiming to make any one group outstandingly happy but to make the whole city so, as far as possible. We thought that we'd find justice most easily in such a city."[110] Not everyone would agree with my analysis of the *Republic*, but I think that it's uncontroversial to say that Plato sought how best to implement justice and the other virtues. The achievement of justice, in my view, is what Plato tried to convey in the *Republic*.

THE STUDENT:

I understand your point of view, without necessarily agreeing with it.[111] But even if Plato is not setting out in the *Republic* a blueprint for a fascist state, and instead trying to set out some analysis of how to achieve justice, what does this imply for bribery?

THE PRIEST:

I support this question. We've heard a compelling and fascinating overview of justice in the Platonic state and the

---

[110] *Republic* 420b.

[111] That there is no consensus on the interpretation of the *Republic* is reflected in the vast and varied secondary literature on the dialogue.

Platonic individual. But it's been a lot to digest, and I think that we need to step back a little, gather our thoughts, and refocus on bribery.

THE CLASSICIST:

Alright. We've seen how bribery violates justice and has a corrupting effect on society. Like the individual man Socrates, the ruling class in the *Republic* avoids bribery of any kind, because the avoidance of bribery is central to a virtuous disposition. In Callipolis, the rulers are deprived of all significant wealth, and the abolition of private property obviously removes one driver of bribery, which is the temptation of the abuse of power for personal gain. A courageous military class and a moderate productive class should also have some virtue-based immunity when it comes bribery so, as a whole, the political dispensation of Callipolis, being based on justice, should be bribery-free. And this ties in with Socrates's moderate disposition, which led him to refuse a bribe to escape his execution. By making these things clear, Plato is conveying the notion that virtue is a kind of knowledge: By using our reason, we can assess the right course of action. This is the lens through which Plato's concept of bribery can be understood: It is an activity that we can rationally assess to reach a conclusion as to its harmfulness.

THE ECONOMIST:

Your point is well taken. But can we move on? Are there other concepts of justice in relation to bribery developed by Plato in his writings? After all, the *Republic* is only one of his dialogues, albeit an important one.

THE CLASSICIST:

Well, the topic of justice runs through Plato's writings, so let's look at some of them. We might start with the *Laws*, widely considered to be Plato's final work, and in my view a corrective to what some perceive as the utopian excesses of the *Republic*. In *Laws*, the city-state of Magnesia is a more practical and realistic alternative to the utopia of Callipolis; there are no extreme or authoritarian measures. Rather, as the title of that dialogue suggests, it's a city governed by laws.

THE PRIEST:

Is there any mention of bribery in the *Laws*?

THE CLASSICIST:

Listen to this passage, which I shall quote verbatim: "Members of the public service should perform their duties without taking bribes. Such a practice must never be extenuated by an approving reference to maxims like 'One good turn deserves another'. It is not easy for an official to reach his decisions impartially and stick to them, and the safest thing he can do is to listen to the law and obey its command and to take no gifts for his service."[112]

THE ECONOMIST:

That's very clear. No ambiguity at all.

THE CLASSICIST:

Correct. The public official is to avoid any dabbling in gifts and bribery. There is simply no room for bribery in Plato's Magnesia, whether at the level of a gargantuan bribe or even a more modest gift. What's more, the penalty for bribery by public officials in Plato's Magnesia is death.[113] There's no

---

[112] *Laws* XII 955c-d.
[113] Athenian law also considered bribery involving senior public officials to be a serious crime. In addition to the death penalty, alternative

doubt about the corrupting effects of bribery on public administration.

THE PRIEST:

That deals with what we'd consider to be the civil service. Is there any mention of bribery in the *Laws* for the general citizen?

THE CLASSICIST:

Of course. Let me again quote from the text: "[T]he pursuit of money should come last in the scale of value. Every man directs his efforts to three things in all, and if his efforts are directed with a correct sense of priorities he will give money the third and lowest place, and his soul the highest, and his body coming somewhere between the two."[114] The lowering of the importance given to money has clear implications for suppressing a culture of bribery.

And, finally, let me draw attention to another aspect of the *Laws*. Plato seems to be establishing for Magnesia a civil theology on the basis that the gods exist, that they care about man, and that they cannot be bribed.

THE PRIEST:

Ah, the theme of bribing the gods.

THE CLASSICIST:

Allow me to give a final quotation from the *Laws*: "No one who believes in gods as the law directs ever voluntarily commits

---

Athenian punishments included exile and a fine of ten times the value of the original bribe. See Gmirkin (2017, 131).

[114] *Laws* V 743e.

an unholy act or lets any lawless word pass his lips. If he does, it is because of one of three possible misapprehensions: either...he believes (1) the gods do not exist, or (2) that they exist but take no thought for the human race, or (3) that they are bribed by sacrifices and supplications and can easily be won over." The punishment Plato envisions under Magnesia's criminal code for such impiety is imprisonment and, following death, burial outside the state's boundaries.[115] Plato seems to have wanted a rational religion to banish from Magnesia the pernicious doctrine of trying to bribe the gods. This brings to mind our earlier discussions[116] on the extent to which Jewish and Christian prayer may be considered a kind of bribery.

I think, at this point, that I'd like to move on from Plato, at least for now. Plato had a lot more to say about justice and the virtues, but I'd like to introduce them, as appropriate, during the rest of our discussions.[117] Now I'd like to turn to what Aristotle had to say.

THE PRIEST:

Plato's most outstanding student. I'd like to hear how Aristotle advanced Plato's theories of the virtues and the implications of this for bribery.

THE CLASSICIST:

I'm not sure I'd agree that Aristotle advanced Plato's ideas on this matter. That would suggest that Plato is somehow incomplete or superseded. Instead, I'd say that Aristotle

---

[115] *Laws* X 885b and 909a–d.

[116] In Section Two.

[117] The classicist seems to be anticipating the discussion of relativism in Section Six.

elaborated very interesting concepts of ethics and that the influence of his viewpoints has been immense.

THE ECONOMIST:

I imagine that our discussions will turn towards the notion of "virtue ethics" as it's often understood today.

THE CLASSICIST:

Indeed. To understand Aristotle's approach in comparison with Plato's, we have only to reflect on a sixteenth-century Vatican fresco by Raphael.[118] Look, I've brought a copy for us to consider. It depicts an elderly Plato walking in conversation with his middle-aged student, Aristotle. Plato points upwards, to the sky, reflecting his emphasis on transcendental, universal realities. In contrast, Aristotle points earthwards, reflecting his interest in empirical realities. Aristotle focused on the day-to-day reality of particulars rather than on the kinds of abstractions that formed the basis of Plato's reality. And look at the book that Raphael has Aristotle carry under his arm: It's his *Nichomachean Ethics*. This shows—does it not?—the importance of Aristotle's writings on ethics. In contrast, Plato is carrying his *Timaeus*, which deals with the nature of the physical world and of humanity.

THE STUDENT:

It might also reflect what was popular and well known at that point in time in the sixteenth century. An author's individual works come and go, in terms of popularity and fashion, and each age has its own favorites.

---

[118] The School of Athens (*La Scuola di Atene*) was completed in the early sixteenth century.

THE CLASSICIST:

Good point. But I maintain that ethics is a significant, enduring part of Aristotle's writings. His *Nicomachean Ethics* is a work of immense importance.

THE ECONOMIST:

And did Aristotle have much to say on bribery?

THE CLASSICIST:

In direct terms, very little. Bribery doesn't figure prominently in Aristotle's surviving writings, but his virtue ethics are certainly applicable to concerns about bribery. Let me offer a very brief summary of the Aristotelian approach to this topic. I mentioned just now that Aristotle tended towards the practical rather than the abstract. In particular, he considered ethics to be a very practical matter. He accepted the cardinal virtues, which he interpreted in terms of the need for correct behavior, and he envisioned correct behavior as having neither an excess nor a deficiency of individual virtues.

THE PRIEST:

You're referring here to the "Golden Mean"?

THE CLASSICIST:

Yes. Aristotle saw proper virtue as a correct measure, or mean, on a continuum between extremes, in the sense of achieving a middle way between the excess or deficiency of a virtue.

THE PRIEST:

So, to put this in concrete terms, let's take the example of courage. Too much courage can amount to recklessness, and too little courage can result in cowardice. A balance is needed. That's the approach we're dealing with, isn't it?

THE CLASSICIST:

Yes. A three-tiered relational structure of a virtue with two corresponding vices, one of excess and one of deficiency, was his broad approach to the virtues.[119] Now, it's also important to realize that Aristotle considered the purpose of human life to be the achievement of what is often translated as "happiness" but which I prefer to call "self-fulfillment".[120] This state of being is the greatest good for Aristotle, and it's achieved by a balanced character with balanced virtues. For Aristotle, self-fulfillment is not achieved by following lists of laws or rules. Instead, it is founded on a general excellence of character.[121] His concept of self-fulfillment amounted to a

---

[119] Had the classicist been so inclined, he might have mentioned Aristotle's differentiation between virtues of character, like courage, and virtues of the intellect, like practical wisdom. He also declines to discuss the distinctions between ethics and morals—the former based on the Greek term *ethos* (ἦθος), meaning "character" or "disposition", and the latter on the Latin *mores*, meaning "customs" or "usage". These omissions may perhaps be a result of the classicist's intention to make his presentation of these topics brief.

[120] The Aristotelian concept of *eudaimonia* (εὐδαιμονία) is often translated as "happiness", but alternatives include "self-fulfillment", "self-actualization", and "virtuous attainment". The concept has nothing to do with fleeting pleasure but is rather a matching of virtues of character with virtues of intellect to achieve a consistently honorable way of living.

[121] The classicist glosses over some of Aristotle's views on *eudaimonia*, perhaps in the interests of keeping the dialogue unencumbered by too many technicalities. For Aristotle, the virtues were necessary but not sufficient for self-fulfillment: He emphasized the importance of other, external "goods" such as friends and wealth in a truly self-fulfilled life. He therefore doubted whether self-fulfillment could be achieved for a person who was "extremely ugly" or who had "totally depraved children or friends, or ones who were good but dead" (*Nichomachean Ethics* 1099b3–8). The classicist does not explore such thoughts in this discussion.

flourishing of the individual and a successful way of living: As he put it, it's "activity of the soul in accordance with excellence".[122]

THE STUDENT:

The soul again! We're back to metaphysical speculation. And didn't Aristotle exclude women and slaves from his ethical concept of the good life? Doesn't this undermine claims that his ethics are a complete and valuable system?

THE CLASSICIST:

First of all, what Aristotle told us can be fully secularized. Talk of the soul was just the convention of his day. As we mentioned with respect to Plato, we can replace "soul" with "consciousness" or "character". Aristotle's personality was very much down-to-earth. He wasn't prone to lofty, metaphysical speculation. The cardinal virtues were the bedrock of Aristotle's notions of virtue, and his self-fulfillment was not envisioned as occurring in isolation but rather at the heart of social interaction.

As for his exclusion of women and slaves, this reflects, it seems to me, the conditions of the times. By today's standards, of course, this is wrong. Later interpreters of Aristotle purged these unacceptable aspects out of his ethics, and I think that his system still survives intact after the purging of these unpleasant elements.

You surely know that Aristotle famously called the human being a political animal.[123] Note that he didn't call the human

---

[122] *Nichomachean Ethics* 1098a16.
[123] *Politics* I 1.1253a2. The concept of the *zōon politikon* (ζῷον πολιτικόν) was also developed in his *History of Animals* I 1.488a8–10.

being a social animal, which is still, today, a common platitude, but rather a *political* animal. Being a political animal implies that one has to learn how to live properly within the formal governance structures of society. The state is not an artificial trapping imposed on us but rather a manifestation of human nature. We therefore need to flourish not only in a social context but also in a political context, and it is in this environment that the virtues can be assessed. For Plato, as we heard, an analysis of virtuous behavior requires the application of reason. Similarly for Aristotle, achieving self-fulfillment requires rational activity.[124] In a political setting, therefore, Aristotle advocates a firmly virtuous disposition, or mindset, that is inculcated by acting in accordance with the virtues.

THE ECONOMIST:

I think I can detect a problem in what you're saying. If our ethical behavior is to be based on a virtuous disposition, then what does this mean for the consequences of our actions?

THE CLASSICIST:

I don't follow.

THE ECONOMIST:

Let's say that I'm self-fulfilled in Aristotle's sense: How should we interpret my actions if I consistently maintain my virtuous disposition? According to what you've been saying, it seems that the consequences of what I do don't really matter, simply

---

[124] Warnock (1998, 107) draws attention to the importance of emotion in supplementing reason in matters ethical: "The proper reaction to a moral wrong is indignation or outrage...The subject-matter of ethics demands that one become emotionally as well as theoretically and philosophically committed to one's beliefs."

because my character has been established as being virtuous. So if you, too, are self-fulfilled but your actions differ fundamentally from mine, who's to say if my actions are more ethical than yours? I can't understand how we can ignore the consequences of actions if we're simply looking at the character of the person who does the action. How, then, do we reconcile the different actions of individuals who may all claim to have good, or self-fulfilled, characters?

THE CLASSICIST:

I see your point now, and it's well expressed. Indeed, this is the reason there are so few advocates today of Aristotle's pure virtue ethics. There is usually some tempering of what Aristotle has to say, which we'll surely discuss in due course.[125] But the whole concept of virtue ethics has much to commend it; it encourages us to avoid extremes, to inculcate good habits of behavior and, more broadly, to reflect on what is morally correct in society.

THE ECONOMIST:

Please allow me to try to fathom the implications of what you've been saying. Virtue ethics seems to be based on one's character. Unlike consequentialist ethical approaches, which are assessed on the outcomes of actions, virtue ethics seem to have a weakness in not ensuring a consistent methodology to assess the value of the results of our actions. So, when it comes to bribery, can we say that bribery is always wrong? Does our ethical assessment of a bribe depend on its consequences? Or does it depend solely on the moral character and the intentions of the people involved in a bribe?

---

[125] In Section Four.

THE CLASSICIST:

Again, I admit you're drawing attention to a weakness of virtue ethics. I'd respond by saying that bribery in the context of virtue ethics must be framed within the cardinal virtues, especially the virtue of justice, alongside the concept of self-fulfillment. Let's take money: Wealth is a means to an end, for Aristotle, and not an end in itself, while self-fulfillment is indeed an end in itself. Therefore, wealth for its own sake is not self-fulfillment.[126] Bribery should be viewed in that context: It's a means to an end, and if the end is the subversion of justice, then it must be wrong.

As for Aristotle's main analysis of justice, we should look to his *Nicomachean Ethics*,[127] where he discusses various meanings of the term, and to *Politics*, where he applies justice in a political context. In *Politics*, he looks at corruption only in a general way. For him, as for Plato, corruption consisted mainly in rulers governing in their self-interest rather than for the common good. Both Plato and Aristotle understood that the appropriate virtues for rulers might differ somewhat from the appropriate virtues for citizens, but in any case, I can't see any support for any forms of bribery in their surviving writings.

---

[126] *Nicomachean Ethics* 1096a5–7.

[127] Mainly in Book V, in which Aristotle discusses justice in a universal sense, related to the other virtues, and in a particularist sense, in which it applies in situations where circumstances may necessitate a technical grasp of the issues involved. Examples of the latter include commercial justice (for economic exchange and matters of fairness), remedial justice (in criminal and civil law, when a wrong has to be remedied) and distributive justice (in the allocation of social benefits and responsibilities). The classicist chooses not to elaborate on these distinctions.

THE ECONOMIST:

Alright. I suggest we now wrap up our discussion of the Greeks, and then we can move on to a discussion of the fusion, or combination, of biblical and Greek ethics in Western culture.

THE STUDENT:

I must voice again my concerns at the ethnocentric path this discussion has taken.

THE ECONOMIST:

I share your concern. But I think it's important, as we said earlier, to discuss how the traditionalist arguments are constructed on the basis of the Jewish and Greek cultural strands being fused together in Christianity to determine European culture, and how they influenced—either directly or by repudiation—the humanist and secular European culture that superseded or accompanied Christianity from the Enlightenment onwards. I'm sure we'll all have plenty to say about these topics.

THE STUDENT:

You're not wrong in saying that!

THE ECONOMIST:

If you permit, I'll summarize our discussions to this point. In terms of what the Bible has to say about bribery and morality, we found that it contained a largely duty-based condemnation of the injustices caused by bribery. Yet we were surprised, or at least I was surprised, that the Bible left open, without condemnation, the practice of gift-giving for minor influencing purposes, where this is simply an accepted social practice. To an extent, one might say that the Bible permits a certain degree of consequentialism in its approach, in that it requires judgment about the consequences of a gift. In other words, does a specific gift subvert justice, or is it simply a social gesture that opens doors to legitimate social and political activity without violating fundamental justice? But I prefer not to exaggerate the consequentialist nature of biblical morality on matters of bribery. It certainly falls far short of the economic consequentialism that I'll be talking of in due course.

With the Greeks, we again saw the condemnation of bribery to the extent that it subverts justice. We have, in Plato and Aristotle, a secular basis for assessing bribery based on the cardinal virtues, of which justice was the most important in relation to bribery. Aristotle developed an intriguing theory about how a virtuous disposition could drive our ethical behavior, but in both Plato and Aristotle I detected little, if anything, in terms of a defense of any form of bribery.

I hope you find this a fair summary of what we've discussed so far. Now, as we agreed, we'll turn our attention to how these two streams of ethics, from the Bible and the Greeks, fused together in Western culture.

THE PRIEST:

I'd say that the Hellenized Christianity that took shape in the Catholic Church essentially married together Judeo-Christian revelation with Greek wisdom. This fusion created what we know today as Western ethics, but it has universal implications. Even with the development of post-Enlightenment secularism, the ethical framework of the Church continues to set the foundation of our understanding of ethics.

THE STUDENT:

I cannot let your comments go unchallenged. From my point of view, there's so much wrong in what you just said that we should unpick carefully the notion of the Church setting universal ethics and of setting the framework for secular ethics.

THE PRIEST:

Then let me make my case, and I'll be happy to defend it.

THE CLASSICIST:

This would be a good approach. Let's hear your arguments and investigate that ancient question: What does Jerusalem have to do with Athens?[128]

---

[128] An allusion to *De praescriptione haereticorum* of Tertullian (c. 155–240 AD), Chapter 7: *Quid Athenae Hierosolymis?*

Chapter Four
Jerusalem and Athens

THE PRIEST:

The supreme entity of Plato's philosophy was the form of the Good. The Good was an abstract reality, not a divine person. It was a secular concept. But later, in marrying the Bible with Greek wisdom, Christianity would associate Plato's form of the Good with God.[129] Let's not forget that Plato and Aristotle were largely forgotten in the West for a thousand years before their "rediscovery", so to speak, in the Middle Ages. But their virtues were kept alive by, and in, the Church. The *Catechism of the Catholic Church* defines "virtue", in terms that strikingly echo Aristotle, as "a habitual and firm disposition to do the good".[130] And Christianity not only accepted the four cardinal virtues of the Greeks, it added some virtues of its own.

THE CLASSICIST:

Which virtues did the Church add to the cardinal virtues?

---

[129] It is uncannily fortuitous that the removal of a single vowel in modern English reflects the change of emphasis from "good" to "God". The speaker seems here to have in mind the Augustinian concept of Plato's forms existing in the mind of God and the notion that Augustine "baptized Platonism" by synthesizing Plato and Christianity: See Kreeft (2018, 45–46).

[130] Section 1803.

THE PRIEST:

There was a long history of debate and development, but to cut a long story short, the three theological virtues of faith, hope, and charity were added to the four classical cardinal virtues of justice, courage, moderation, and wisdom. In total, therefore, there are seven virtues in the Church.[131] Of course, the three theological virtues were considered to be different from the secular, classical virtues on the grounds of their divine inspiration.[132] And I must point out that the theological virtues not only have a different status from the cardinal virtues, but they do not have equal status among themselves. Charity is considered to be the most important, based on Saint Paul's comments in the New Testament.[133] I could talk at length about the unity of the Greek and the theological virtues and the relationships between them because it's a fascinating subject, but I'd like to focus specifically on bribery.

THE ECONOMIST:

Yes, I'm eager to hear how the unified virtues of the Church treat bribery.

THE PRIEST:

Then let's state that, *prima facie*, the two virtues most violated by an act of bribery are justice and charity. Therefore, we

---

[131] See the summary of the virtues in the second part of the *Summa Theologica* of Thomas Aquinas (1225–1274).

[132] *Catechism*, Sections 1840–1841: "The theological virtues...have God for their origin, their motive, and their object...They inform all the moral virtues and give life to them."

[133] The virtue of charity can also be translated into English as "love". In 1 *Corinthians* 13, Paul emphasizes the supremacy of love (Greek *agape*, ἀγάπη, and Latin *caritas*, from which the English "charity"): "...faith, hope and love abide, these three; and the greatest of these is love".

have one of the Greek virtues and one of the theological virtues to consider. We've already discussed justice in the context of Plato and Aristotle. I'll quote from the *Catechism* to give the Church's definition of justice: It "consists in the firm and constant will to give God and neighbor their due".[134] We can see, in the words "firm and constant", the link with the Aristotelian concept of the virtuous disposition. The Catechism also tells us the following: "By charity, we love God above all things and our neighbor as ourselves for love of God. Charity, the form of all the virtues, 'binds everything together in perfect harmony'".[135] The bribe, as we have already seen, violates justice, and the bribe also violates charity, as it is the opposite of the charitable gift.

THE ECONOMIST:

And in practice? How did the Church handle bribery during the centuries it held, or dominated, temporal as well as spiritual power?

THE PRIEST:

A great question. As we heard earlier, the New Testament contains almost no discussion of bribery in abstract terms. It does, however, provide specific examples in its narratives of human actions as paradigms of good or bad behavior. We saw how Saint Paul resisted a bribe, how Judas took a bribe to betray Christ, and how the Roman soldiers were bribed to cover up the Resurrection. These examples are meant to guide our behavior. I think the lack of abstract discussion of bribery in the New Testament reflects not only the earlier coverage of this topic in the Old Testament but also

---

[134] Section 1836.

[135] Section 1844. The New Testament quotation embedded in this definition refers to *Colossians* 3:14.

the fact that the early Christians held little power; they were initially a countercultural movement that was persecuted and oppressed. Only later, when the Roman Empire adopted Christianity as its official religion, was the Church required to really confront the issue in detail.[136]

THE CLASSICIST:

Indeed! Being in opposition and being in power are very different. It's little wonder that the Church had eventually to address this matter head-on, once it took power.

THE PRIEST:

Absolutely. The example of an attempt to solicit bribery in the New Testament that is most relevant to our discussion is that of Simon the Magician. As we heard earlier, he unsuccessfully tried to bribe the apostles. Simon the Magician gave his name to simony, the purchase and sale of holy orders that roiled the medieval Church. Simony was an affront to the virtues of the Church, and it was a form of bribery that corrupted the Church at the highest levels.[137] It led to centuries of argument, debates, and attempted reform that flared around this issue.[138]

---

[136] Compare Noonan (1984, 55–56): "The problems [of bribery] are more apparent in the fourth century, when the Christians came to power, than in the first century."

[137] Dante placed Simon and some of his fellow simonists in the eighth circle of his hell in the *Divina Commedia*, only one circle higher than Judas. This is indicative of the gravity of simony in the Church. Simon and his companions are kept upside down in Dante's hell, reflecting their inversion of ethical practices. See ns. 58 and 73. Modern bribery in public life may perhaps be seen as a secular version of ecclesiastical simoniac practices.

[138] For example, the reforms of Pope Innocent III (1160–1216) at the Fourth Lateran Council.

THE STUDENT:

So much for religion. I think we need also to consider secular ethics.

THE PRIEST:

In my understanding, modern secular ethics in the West is derived from the seven virtues of the Church of the Middle Ages.

THE STUDENT:

That seems like a big claim, if not a preposterous one. What about the humanists and the Enlightenment?

THE PRIEST:

Allow me to summarize my understanding of the topic as follows. In the Middle Ages, if I might simplify things greatly, the Church was a sacramental organization that mediated divine grace to individuals. It had, more or less, a monopoly in terms of ethics. The Church, however, started to experience serious challenges, especially from about 1200 onwards. Groups like the Cathars, an offshoot of the Bogomils,[139] contested the Church's institutional dominance, and while the suppression of such movements worked in the short term, the eventual result was the schism in Western Christianity that led to the Reformation. In turn, the Renaissance and the Enlightenment secularized large parts of life in the West, including the sphere of ethics.

---

[139] The Bogomils were a dualist sect originating in the tenth century in the First Bulgarian Empire. One of their offshoot movements was that of the Cathars, or Albigensians, in southern France (and northern Italy). The movement was violently suppressed by the Church.

All this amounted to a major cultural transformation, but behind these monumental changes there was hidden a basic, underlying continuity. It may be tempting to see modern secular ethics as a break from the Christian past, but in truth they are essentially reworkings of Christian ethics. I'd say that the Church's ethical system continues to be alive and well in the Church, obviously, while the secular world experiences it as a kind of permanent afterglow. Socialists, for example, base their ethics on virtues like justice and charity. Secular conservatives base their ethics more on moderation and faith. The ethics of the Church have simply been rephrased in secular terms. To use an old analogy, what we've seen is the putting of old wine into new bottles.

THE STUDENT:

That's a very controversial standpoint, if you don't mind me saying so, in terms of a genealogy of ethics. There's much that is wrong, it seems to me, in what you're saying. You surely can't be telling us that modern ethics, such as it is, is simply a secularized form of Christian ethics?

THE PRIEST:

Well, basically, yes, that's what I'm saying.

THE STUDENT:

Then you seem to be saying that ethics today in the West is the result of a simple tale of ancient Jewish moral codes in a dialectical relationship with the Platonic virtues, and somehow the Church brought all this together, and now we can't escape from it all?

THE PRIEST:

There are some qualifications to make but, essentially, that's indeed correct. Medieval Christians and modern ideologues have a lot more in common than first meets the eye. There has been a process of the de-divinization of ethics rather than a fundamental transformation. The ancient virtues live on through the spiritual disorder of our times, whether in the ideological pathologies of modernism or in the nihilism of the postmodernists. The saints of the Church are analogous to the heroes of the secular revolutions, and sin has turned into whatever activity contradicts the latest party or ideological line.

THE STUDENT:

Seriously?

THE PRIEST:

Most seriously! Modern ideology is largely a perversion of Christianity. The concept of the righteous in the Church's teachings was twisted into the proletariat in Communism and into the white race in Nazism. The secular versions of hell were the gulags and concentration camps. What we've experienced is a deformation of Christian spirituality, and it has caused untold harm in the modern world. The murder of God by secularists has led to genocide and evil on an immense scale. The spiritual and intellectual decay of the West can best be seen in the modern Academy, which is prey both to sick ideologies and reality-denying nihilism. The university is no longer an institution that searches for truth: It's been deformed into a mechanism for the dissemination of evil.

THE STUDENT:

Whoa! This seems like abuse, not discussion.

THE CLASSICIST:

Let's restrain ourselves a little at this point. I'm sure our friend is not being abusive but simply setting out concrete descriptions of the truth, as he sees it. What I think is being conveyed here is the notion that, when severed from their theological roots, the classical and theological virtues can become dangerous because they're unrestrained by the cultural forces that nurtured them. One might think, for example, of the French revolutionaries who, drunk with their visions of justice, ended up committing mass slaughter in the name of that virtue.

THE STUDENT:

I'm well aware that some reactionary worldviews remain wedded to outdated traditions, but I have what I believe to be a very coherent argument to counter them.

THE ECONOMIST:

I understand your concerns, and I know you must be finding it frustrating because right now your contributions are limited mainly to reactions to the topics under discussion. But I assure you that we shall end with your segment, so to speak.[140]

THE STUDENT:

(Laughs). So you'll permit the *soixante-huitarde*[141] to speak, eventually?

---

[140] In Section Six.
[141] See n. 11.

THE ECONOMIST:

(Also laughs). Most assuredly.

THE STUDENT:

Then perhaps I should be pleased at that. But, frankly, I don't think it's right for you to try to postpone my contribution to the end of the discussion. Are we not in a dialogue, a dialectical process of give and take? If you silence my perspective now, you'll simply allow your grand narratives to flow unchallenged. Permitting me to jump in only at the end is hardly a fair approach to our discussions.

THE CLASSICIST:

I agree. It's not enough for you to have a promise that you'll have the last word in our discussions. Your arguments must be heard throughout all stages of our conversation. We must conduct these discussions in the spirit of a free exchange of ideas. As an economist who believes in the value of competition, you must surely accept the value of an open market in competitive ideas?

THE ECONOMIST:

(After a brief pause). Of course. You're right. You're totally right. I must apologize for trying to arrange our discussions too rigidly. My only intention was to try to manage the flow of our meeting, but I can see that I was wrong to try to stifle any contributions that any of us may wish to make at any point. My intentions were good, but my handling of the situation was bad. Please accept my apology and proceed. The health of our discussions depends on us hearing your objections to anything that's been said so far.

THE STUDENT:

Apology accepted. I do have plenty to say. Fundamentally, I object to the kind of reactionary narratives we've been discussing up to this point. I feel I must intervene when I hear something so ludicrous that I can't let it pass.

THE CLASSICIST:

Naturally.

THE STUDENT:

Then I shall draw attention to the narrative of the Jewish and Greek roots of Western civilization. There's so much to unpack here that it's almost hard for me to know where to begin. I could start with the Jewish and Christian background, where I perceive an ill-defined cultural appropriation of other cultures, but I prefer to focus on the Greeks. I find it astonishing that the self-appointed spokesmen of the West, and they are indeed mainly men, claim the ancient Greeks as their cultural ancestors. There's plenty of evidence to support contrary notions.

THE CLASSICIST:

Please tell us more.

THE STUDENT:

We live now in a postmodern and postcolonial world, and the old narratives are breaking down. The idea that the West is the direct descendent of Greek antiquity doesn't, in my opinion, bear scrutiny. It's an ideological construct that's used by some to justify traditionalist discourses of Western power, white supremacy, and the denigration of what is considered to be "the Other".

THE PRIEST:

You're making very large claims! Haven't I shown how the West developed its culture, mediated by the Church, by means of a fusion of the Bible and Greek culture?

THE STUDENT:

That is certainly one narrative, but I'm challenging that narrative as being ideological. Your narrative isn't the truth: It's only one narrative among many others. You claim that the modern West is a descendent of the Greece of antiquity, with a genealogy channeled through certain canonical books and through institutions like the Church, with the result that we are the proud inheritors of the world's finest traditions of politics, ethics, philosophy, and the like. This so-called continuity is, in fact, not at all clear. First, the Greeks were in many ways an alien culture, as different from what is now the West as were the ancient Jews. The West likes to see the ancient Greeks as its ancestors, but in fact it takes a lot of intellectual gymnastics to reconcile the Hellenic culture with our modern Western culture. For example, there is a convincing counter-narrative that the Greeks mediated African culture to the West, so our much-vaunted reliance on the Greek heritage might actually be a misappropriation of an African heritage.

THE PRIEST:

An African heritage? What do you mean?

THE CLASSICIST:

There's a long-running scholarly debate over the origins of Greek culture. Some allege that, in a similar manner to the Roman appropriation of Greek culture, the Greeks had earlier appropriated African culture, mediated through Egypt.[142] And, the story goes, Western scholars have turned a blind eye to the African origins of Greek culture to promote a narrative of African backwardness in contrast to Western progressivism.

THE PRIEST:

Is this hypothesis credible? Or is it just empty bluster?

THE CLASSICIST:

In my opinion, it's not credible. There was certainly some cross-fertilization of Mediterranean cultures in antiquity, but, to me, the notion that the Greeks misappropriated or hijacked African culture is, frankly, ludicrous.

THE STUDENT:

Of course you'd say that. The West's investment in its monolithic narrative of the ancient Greeks as being Europeans, and descriptions of their achievements as being purely *sui generis* and without outside influence, are so deep that the Afrocentric counter-narrative shakes it to its roots. Western discourses around the slave trade and other racist and unethical behavior depend on the narrative of a direct Western descent from Greek antiquity. And there are additional narratives out there, too, which deserve our attention. Some see

---

[142] Major landmarks in the Afrocentric analysis of ancient Greek culture are James (1954) and the multi-volume Bernal (1987).

Indian influences on Greek philosophy, for example, in the theories like the transmigration of souls that were advanced by Plato, among others.

THE ECONOMIST:

However fascinating ancient Mediterranean culture is, I'm struggling to see what this line of argument has to do with our discussion of bribery. I fear our conversation is running into a risk of derailment.

THE STUDENT:

Well, I think that we've based our understandings of the ethics of bribery on false narratives, and that means we're basing our discussions on shaky foundations. So we may invoke the ancient Greeks when it suits us or perhaps denounce their heritage as Orientalist[143] when it doesn't suit our purposes, but should our arguments really depend so heavily on the unstable basis of heritage politics?[144]

THE CLASSICIST:

It's not necessary to exaggerate the problem. I don't think our analysis of the influence of Greek virtues on Western culture in necessarily undermined by any Afrocentric or other theory about the origins of Greek achievements.

---

[143] A reference to the line of literary and social criticism articulated by Said (1978), in which Western presumptions of cultural superiority color perceptions of the "East" along clichéd and stereotypical lines.

[144] Hanink (2017, 28) provides a striking example of a modern denial of Greek "Westernness", quoting Valéry Giscard d'Estaing, former president of France, as saying, in 2001, in relation to Greece's entry into the Euro currency zone: "To be perfectly frank, it was a mistake to accept Greece [into the Eurozone]. Greece simply wasn't ready. Greece is basically an Oriental country."

THE PRIEST:

I agree. My arguments have rested on the outcomes of the Greek virtues, not on their origins.

THE ECONOMIST:

Alright. I think we need to acknowledge the contested narratives that surround the origins of ancient Greek culture. But for the purposes of our review of bribery, let me try to summarize where our discussions have reached. Also, please permit me to say that I share the concerns about the validity today of some of the traditional discourses we've heard. I'm no believer in divine commands or Platonic Forms, and in no way did I wish to brush aside any challenges to these ways of thinking. All our voices must be heard in full: That is the only way our discussions will achieve their full potential.

So, in discussing the development of ethics in the West, we talked, I think, about the Western system of ethics having its roots in both the biblical and classical worlds.

THE STUDENT:

That's true for the traditional narrative of Western ethics.

THE ECONOMIST:

Correct. Then we discussed how the Reformation and then the secularization process first diversified the Church's medieval religious monopoly and then broke it, at least in a formal sense. Of course, the religious narrative continues, and with vigor, at least for those prepared to hear it, but alternative voices and discourses have arisen that our consideration of bribery must take in account.

We've heard duty-based arguments, based on divine commands in the Bible, which portray actions as intrinsically moral or immoral in themselves, largely irrespective of their consequences. I personally was a little surprised at the flexibility of the Bible's commands on bribery. Nonetheless, the kind of gift-giving that subverts justice is condemned as bribery in the Bible because God, or someone speaking on God's behalf, has decreed that it is wrong.

THE PRIEST:

But let's not forget that there's a role for rationality in interpreting and applying biblical ethics. It's not simply blind submission to a set of rules.

THE ECONOMIST:

Quite. And we also discussed the virtue ethics of the classical world. These ethics are largely character-based ethics, in that the determination of whether an act is moral or immoral is based on the character trait that the act exhibits. The strength of virtue ethics, it seems to me, is in its emphasis on the need to develop virtuous habits. An understanding of what is virtuous is not enough; what we need is hard work and application. On the other hand, a weakness of this way of thinking is that it doesn't set out clear rules on how to behave, which is very much contrary to the deontological or duty-based approach.

I propose that we now move on to consider consequentialist ethics. As its name suggests, this is an approach in which an act is considered to be moral or immoral on the basis of its outcomes. If I give gifts or bribes to soldiers in a war setting, with the intention of keeping innocent people safe from a genocide, in the manner of Oskar Schindler,[145] then surely such a bribe must be seen as virtuous. So, it seems to me, it makes no sense to declare bribery to always be immoral if sometimes it can have good consequences.[146] Of course, in my discussions the focus will be on economic factors, and on the costs, if any, of small bribery, and I hope to persuade you of the validity of my views.

THE PRIEST:

With some small reservations, I can accept this as a brief summary of where our discussions have brought us and where they need to go next.

THE CLASSICIST:

Then let's hear the consequentialist arguments from your economic viewpoint.

---

[145] The bribes paid by Oskar Schindler are discussed by Nichols (2015).

[146] Velasquez (2012, 477) suggests that corruption "can inflict significant costs on society, but not every individual act of corruption does so". Nichols (2015, 675) refers to various good purposes for which bribes may be paid in authoritarian societies: "...so that people may engage in activities such as practicing a religion, secretly learning to read, bartering and exchanging goods, or visiting family".

Chapter Five
The Economics of Bribery

THE ECONOMIST:

I'll be pleased briefly to summarize and expand on the arguments I made earlier.[147] If I may use a classical analogy, I think that my arguments will expand our perspectives beyond some of the Procrustean beds we've encountered so far in our discussions.[148] The fundamental insights I'd like to contribute today derive from economics, which, from the perspective of a behavioral science, provides us with an objective basis to analyze the incentives for giving gifts and making bribes.[149] In our discussions of the Bible, though less so with classical Athens, I think we encountered ample support for my basic starting point that there is nothing intrinsically wrong with gift-giving to influence others. I've learned that even prayer is a form of gift for the religiously inclined, provided that it

---

[147] "Earlier": In the opening pages of Section One. In Section Five, the economist is far more prudent in differentiating between gifts and bribes than he was in Section One, presumably because of the impact of the intervening discussions.

[148] Procrustes, in Greek mythology, was a bandit who forced his victims to fit the dimensions of an iron bed, either by cutting off or stretching their limbs. By extension, "Procrustean" refers to an attempt to tailor facts to fit preconceived theories.

[149] Compare Rose-Ackerman (1999, xi): "...an economic approach is fundamental to understanding where corrupt incentives are the greatest".

is not offered with the intention of gaining special favors, at which point a prayer might indeed be considered a bribe.

Going a little deeper into my arguments, I have to emphasize that, as an economist, I study the operation of markets. It seems to me that gifts can be mechanisms of efficiency, especially in the context of inefficient markets, because they are rooted in the kinds of social cooperation and competition that allow markets to function. In the same way that the price mechanism distils immense quantities of social knowledge that help us to establish optimum prices, a small gift also acts as an economic signal that provides nonviolent solutions to economic problems. Modest bribes intended to brush away a very minor misdemeanor, or to make a legitimate transaction move faster, should be considered not only harmless but also a source of social order. We are dealing with a rational choice that responds to real, existing conditions.

THE PRIEST:

It sounds as though you're making excuses for selfish and unethical behavior.

THE ECONOMIST:

That's not at all my intention. Let me elaborate: I'm talking about gifts and what many may call small bribes, not major acts of corruption, and I like to focus on the context of a market that is dysfunctional. There is indisputable evidence that gifts are embedded in the fabric of society. Gifts solidify reciprocal relationships. They're intrinsic to the human condition not only in social interactions but also in the exchange and accumulation of resources. Where price signals function inadequately, or where markets are distorted in other ways, the gift can act as a smoothing mechanism to make things work. I'm not blind, however, to the damage caused by large-scale bribery. I accept that such bribery can distort and ruin both an economy and people's lives. That's why, in our definition, we insisted on "minor, influence-peddling gifts".[150]

THE CLASSICIST:

If I've understood correctly, your arguments advocate some small bribes on the grounds of efficiency or expediency.

THE ECONOMIST:

My arguments are based only partly on efficiency. From a wider viewpoint, they're essentially based on consequences, and efficiency is only one possible consequence among many. Now, the consequences of an action may be positive, negative, or neutral. Markets are mechanisms to harness our self-interest for the general good. Participants in a market seek to maximize their self-interest, and markets tend to channel this individual self-interest in a good direction that benefits the majority. And gifts can be part of this, especially in an inefficient market where processes are arbitrary or distorted in some way.

THE CLASSICIST:

I think I see your point. It's possible that bribes may enhance the efficiency of individual transactions, especially when a market is imperfect. In other words, when a market fails to channel self-interest for productive purposes, the gift-giver can step in to speed things up. Indeed, in some cases, giving gifts can be simply a way of surviving in a tough environment.[151] But what concerns me is that, while the speeding up of individual transactions may indeed be helpful for those

---

[150] See Section One.

[151] Compare Rose-Ackerman (1999, 225): "In a repressive state, where many policies are harmful to all except a favored elite, corruption may be a survival strategy."

individual transactions, they may harm the wider social and economic conditions. It seems to me that widespread bribery is likely to degrade the general conditions and, as I think we said earlier,[152] rent-seeking behavior may flourish, and society as a whole is likely to suffer from a wider degradation.[153]

THE ECONOMIST:

It very much depends on the context.

THE CLASSICIST:

Yes, but allow me to push forward my line of thinking a little more. I'm thinking on my feet, I admit, but I can see some potentially serious flaws in your argument. A gift, or bribe, I agree, can smooth the efficiency of a transaction, much as oil lubricates a clunky machine. However, I would question the overall efficiency gains in contexts of systemic bribery, not least because the recipients of potential bribes would be incentivized deliberately to stall economic activity so as to create extra red tape. By frustrating transactions with a view to soliciting bribes, this class of corrupt individuals is likely to increase delays to overall economic activity. Therefore, it appears to me, economic activity as a whole will be depressed and slowed down by a culture of bribery.

THE PRIEST:

You make a good point.

---

[152] See n. 12.

[153] Fisman and Golden (2017, 3–4 and 83–119) summarize the ways in which corruption might undermine economic, social, and political well-being.

THE ECONOMIST:

I maintain that whether we interpret a gift as a harmless social act or a destructive bribe depends on the consequences. We're dealing with empirical problems and not with religious or philosophical purity. If the consequence of gift-giving is to damage society, for example by increasing bureaucratic red tape, then it cannot be advocated. But if it adds to society's well-being, then I think it can be defended. We may have utopian ideas of reforming all markets to be efficient, and we may have idealistic intentions to outlaw all bribery, but until such a day arrives, I think we have to accept and recognize the value of gifts and small bribes.[154] Working in the private sector, as I have done, I see such challenges frequently.

THE STUDENT:

When you say that gifts and small bribes may be economically acceptable or even desirable in some societies, what societies do you have in mind? Non-Western ones, I presume?

THE ECONOMIST:

I think that the developing world, as a whole, has greater problems with market imperfections, and this in turn seems to necessitate a certain amount of gift-giving in such societies. Or perhaps it's the other way around: Gift-giving is

---

[154] Velasquez (2012, 488) suggests four criteria to make morally permissible "facilitating" or "grease" payments (i.e. small bribes) to low-level officials for the purpose of ensuring that the official performs his or her routine duties: "(1) the person being bribed has an institutional obligation to provide the service for which he or she is being paid, (2) the person paying the official is entitled to the services and so is not asking the official to, say, lie or steal for him, (3) the person making the payment will suffer a relatively significant harm or major inconvenience if the service is not rendered, and (4) making this particular payment will have relatively insignificant costly consequences for society."

a global cultural phenomenon, and the countries in which these practices are most entrenched seem to have the more severely stunted markets. Whatever the cause, the correlation is clear.

THE STUDENT:

I seem to be hearing something akin to cultural imperialism: the civilized "us" and the backward "other".

THE ECONOMIST:

Allow me to express my point of view this way: There are certain countries, mainly the English-speaking ones but also others in northern Europe, in which society and culture have acquired or developed certain attributes that encourage the rule of law, open markets, democratic institutions, and strong systems of accountability for those in public life.[155] All these elements are indispensable to an efficient economic system that doesn't need pervasive gift-giving. The rest of the world, it seems, tends largely to default to gifts, patronage, and influence peddling in order for their societies to function. And when people live under autocratic governments, the officials of the state have significant power: The consequences

---

[155] This pithy summary of "Western" attributes for economic and social advancement bears a similarity with the list provided by North et al (2009) to explain the success of the West in passing from a "limited access" to an "open access" society: (1) an expanding economy, (2) a vibrant and institutionally rich civil society, (3) a powerful, decentralized government that operates with the consent of the governed, and (4) strong impersonal forces that govern social relations, like the rule of law and property rights. This may be compared to the three elements of a modern political order suggested by Fukuyama (2011): (1) a strong and capable state, (2) the subordination of the state to the rule of law, and (3) government accountability to all citizens. Ferguson (2011) proposes six "killer applications" to explain the West's success in recent centuries: (1) competition, (2) science, (3) democracy, (4) medicine, (5) consumerism, and (6) a strong work ethic.

are significant costs that can be imposed by delaying trans-actions, and lucrative bribes that can be extorted.[156] I wish things were otherwise, but they're not.

THE STUDENT:

Like you, I recognize how cultural differences drive social behavior. But I'm uncomfortable at the implications that we're somehow culturally superior to the rest of the world. You seem to be saying that bribes are unacceptable in our civilized part of the world, but we can tolerate them in so-called backward cultures.[157] Your discourse is a fig leaf to cover the promotion of Western dominance and an unwarranted imposition of Western values. And what about Italy? Are we not an example of a kleptocracy? When in Rome, should we do as the Romans do?[158]

THE ECONOMIST:

That's a parody of my viewpoint. You're putting all kinds of insulting words into my mouth.

THE STUDENT:

Alright. Then can you tell us how Italy fits into your "West and the rest" worldview?

---

[156] Khalil et al (2010) discuss trade-offs between noncoercive bribery and extortion and argue that the deterrence of the latter may make bribery a more optimal solution in weakly governed societies.

[157] Theobald (1999) questions as unhelpful and misleading the assumptions underpinning conventional differentiations between neo-patrimonial states (in which an elite abuses the resources of the state to secure the loyalty of "clients" among the citizens) and modern states (in which state resources are used largely for the common good).

[158] An ironic use of a proverb traditionally attributed to Saint Ambrose (c. 340–397).

THE ECONOMIST:

In terms of bribery, Italy is clearly a state that lies somewhere between the "West and the rest", to use your phrase. Italy has had profound problems of public corruption, which are obvious to all, despite it being notoriously difficult to measure corrupt practices like bribery.[159] We certainly, as a nation, might look rather corrupt alongside, say, England or Sweden, but we're nowhere near the level of corruption of some parts of the world. You seem to be suggesting that I have a binary view of the world. In truth, there's something of a continuum of corruption.

THE STUDENT:

Just to make sure I've understood correctly, are you saying that bribery is justifiable in markets that don't work properly or are somehow stunted? But if a market is efficient, then the price mechanism is enough, and bribery isn't needed?

THE ECONOMIST:

That's an oversimplification. My view is that in a situation where a market is inefficient, there are grounds for accepting the validity of gifts and small bribes to make life livable. But I do not condone major bribery. I gave earlier the example of a police official accepting a bribe: In my view, in some contexts, we can legitimately turn a blind eye to a small bribe intended to evade a minor traffic offense, like a parking ticket. In contrast, we are forced to condemn the bribe to the police official that results in a serious criminal going unpunished because the consequences of this are damage

---

[159] On the topic of the difficulty of documenting and tracking bribery, Fisman and Miguel (2008, 18) note that "if bribe takers and givers are doing a halfway decent job of it, there's no obvious paper trail of what took place".

to public confidence in the justice system and the betrayal of the victims of crime.

THE PRIEST:

It seems that your consequentialist approach to gifts and bribes requires a fair amount of judgment. And on what does this judgment rely? How do you differentiate between a helpful gift and a harmful bribe?

THE ECONOMIST:

I don't pretend that it's simple to work out the consequences of economic behavior. I think we should look at individual cases and assess the extent to which they contribute to human happiness. Such assessments are often more qualitative than quantitative.

THE CLASSICIST:

I assume that your economic happiness is not the same as Aristotle's concept of self-fulfillment.[160]

THE ECONOMIST:

It's nothing so lofty and highfalutin as what Aristotle had in mind. I'm talking of the satisfaction of human needs: in short, what economists call "utility".

THE STUDENT:

Aha! So you're talking about utilitarianism: choosing actions that, allegedly, maximize happiness or pleasure.

---

[160] See n. 120.

THE ECONOMIST:

Absolutely.

THE CLASSICIST:

The origins of such views have a long history. In the classical world, Epicurus[161] considered worldly happiness, or rather pleasure, to be the major goal of life.

THE ECONOMIST:

By "utilitarianism", I'm thinking of what was developed in more recent times, mainly in England.[162]

THE PRIEST:

Can you tell us more about utility: what it is, and how it's supposed to be measured?

THE ECONOMIST:

I'll try my best. Put simply, utility is the direct consequence of an action or policy, and it measures the overall goodness of the outcomes.

THE PRIEST:

Please be more specific on what you mean by goodness. Are you talking of physical or economic pleasure? Social justice?

---

[161] Epicurus (341–270 BCE).

[162] Apparently a reference to the development of "classical utilitarianism" in the writings of Jeremy Bentham (1748–1832), John Stuart Mill (1806–1873), and Henry Sidgwick (1838–1900).

Or does it all boil down to a cost/benefit analysis? Can you give examples?

THE ECONOMIST:

In my understanding, collective utility is whatever is good, overall, for the happiness of the majority. By happiness I don't mean a narrow hedonism but rather human well-being in the broadest sense. This may encompass material well-being and prosperity, good health, environmental protection, and political freedom. These things, I admit, are difficult to measure,[163] but what ethical system doesn't involve difficult judgments?

In modern economic analysis, the concept of utility tends to be framed in terms of preference orderings rather than on any alleged eternal truths or divine commands. What's good is what is agreed by convention in, let us say, the social contract we all live under. The notion of utility is socially negotiated and, therefore, it can change over time as society changes, and of course it can differ between societies.

Specifically in terms of bribery, I would consider two consequences of the utilitarian approach to gifts: They make markets efficient, so that they lower overall costs to society,[164] with the ultimate outcome of increased prosperity. So, excluding of course major bribery that causes severe injustice, I would argue that, in some societies, gifts and low-level bribes clear markets quickly, resulting in a more efficient economy and increased prosperity, to the benefit of

---

[163] The speaker has in mind, perhaps, Bentham's attempts to establish a "felicific calculus" to measure happiness.

[164] Rose-Ackerman (1999, 9ff) identifies an additional area of possible economic advantage arising from gift-giving and bribery: In addition to clearing markets and lowering costs, she also draws attention to the role of bribes in acting as "incentive bonuses" to market participants. The latter topic is not covered in the present discussion.

the majority. I think it's safe to assume, therefore, that the consequences of some bribes can be positive overall.[165]

THE CLASSICIST:

I understand your point about efficiency, but our assessment of bribery cannot be driven solely by the logic of abstract economic concepts. Personally, I would classify bribes, even small ones, as a form of economic pathology. They are acts of sacrificing truth to economic expediency. You're simply turning a blind eye to immoral acts so that transactions move along a little quicker. As I mentioned earlier, I think that this can have a corrosive effect on social ethics as a whole, and surely it also has a corrosive effect on the economy.[166]

THE STUDENT:

As far as I'm concerned, I'm pleased that our discussions have moved on from religious dogma, Platonic mumbo-jumbo, and other forms of hokum. I'm therefore delighted to hear arguments that are focused on human realities, whether negotiated with, or imposed by, social conditions. I agree with you that such attitudes vary between societies.

---

[165] Leff (1964) suggests that bribe-taking bureaucrats can play a positive economic role by sabotaging badly designed regulations. He gives the example of the subversion through bribery of dangerous food price controls in Brazil in the 1960s: The bribes may have benefited the country by ensuring a smoother supply of food and thereby reducing malnutrition. Johnsen (2009), using the distribution of automobiles as an example, argues that the consumer can benefit from the efficiencies provided by bribery. Positive side effects of bribery have also been discussed by Colombatto (2003).

[166] Velasquez (2012, 484–485) summarizes empirical evidence that corruption has a negative impact on rates of investment, and that the higher a country's level of corruption, the lower its rate of economic growth. See also Sanyal and Samanta (2010).

However, as I stated right at the start of our conversation,[167] I think your approach fails to protect the weak and the marginalized. Under utilitarianism, good consequences are viewed in terms of the impact on the majority. But what about vulnerable minorities? One must remember that power relations might be reinforced by bribery to protect illegitimate hierarchies of social dominance. By definition, bribes are made and received by those who control the levers of the economy. Corruption therefore channels resources to the personal enrichment of already entrenched elites.

So I ask: What does it matter if bribery smooths economic machinery if a social underclass has to carry the costs of this? It seems to me that economic incentives in a system riddled with bribery are likely to be harmful to minority and marginalized groups, and the resulting inequalities are very likely to be unacceptable.

THE PRIEST:

For my part, what concerns me in your economics-based account is the way utilitarian considerations appear to be severed from the types of morality we've discussed so far. The bribery transaction is at the mercy of whoever is in a position to declare the benefits of its consequences. I don't see a firm basis for the assessment of utility. It seems safe to assume that utilitarianism is based on observers' subjective opinions and not on any sound, underlying rationale.[168] I refer back to our earlier discussions on biblical ethics: The Bible, I continue to argue, opens our minds and hearts to the

---

[167] In Section One.

[168] Compare Scruton (2007, 716): "[A] general difficulty for consequentialist doctrines...is that they describe, not the moral reasoning of the agent, but moral rationalizations of the observer, and hence provide no guide to action".

recuperation of what we may have lost in the empty materialism of modern, utilitarian calculations.

And there's another consideration, too. Sometimes bribery is a primary, immoral act in itself. At other times, it may be a secondary act. For example, if I bribe a police official to avoid a speeding ticket, the original crime was speeding, and bribery is just another layer of immoral activity to cover up the main crime.[169] So bribery may involve layers of immorality. We can't just brush off bribery as a means of speeding up a sluggish economic system.

THE ECONOMIST:

In my defense, I'd say first of all that the utilitarian approach has a very strong advantage: It offers comparative assessments of value. I accept that the measurement of utility can be tricky and that it's often dependent on preference orderings. It's not rooted in biblical commands or Platonic Forms, but I'd argue that this is its strength. Utilitarianism is grounded in the real world, and it's determined by socially agreed conventions that reflect local conditions, not universalist aspirations, and these conventions may change over time to meet social needs.

THE STUDENT:

So you're saying that utility is not based on divine or absolutist moral claims. I can go along with that. But I come back to the issue of protecting the vulnerable. Aren't they simply left behind in your system so long as the majority feels satisfied and happy? Or let me put it another way: If what is perceived as the overall common good is increased, are we willing to tolerate injustice to the minority? After all, we use the term

---

[169] On bribery as a secondary offense, see Samuel (2017).

"white collar crime" to describe acts like bribery; these are crimes that tend to benefit men in suits, not the weakest in society.[170]

THE ECONOMIST:

That's not necessarily so. There are streams of utilitarian theory that have safeguards built in to protect the vulnerable.

THE STUDENT:

How?

THE ECONOMIST:

The good can be defined not simply as the best outcome for the majority but as the consequence that maximizes the distribution of assets and income for the worst off in society.[171] Utility can therefore be measured in terms of the impact on the most vulnerable and not simply on the majority.

---

[170] Sociologist Edwin H. Sutherland (1883–1950) coined the term "white collar crime" and defined it as "crime committed by a person of respectability and high social status in the course of his occupation" (Brioschi, 2017, 183). Croall (2001, 6–11 and 17) queries the fuzziness of definitions of white collar crime, owing to its complexity and the difficult relationship to class and social status, but argues that its use is justified on the grounds of "public and academic resonance".

[171] There seems to be some affinity between the economist's argument and the "maximin" approach put forward by John Rawls (1921–2002), notably in his *A Theory of Justice* (1971), in which alternatives to courses of action are ranked in accordance with the worst possible outcomes in order to select the course of action that maximizes the worst outcome's utility. Rawls elevated the principle of justice over the principle of utility by maximizing the prospects of the least well-off in society. (He also drew attention to the relations between what is right and what is good: In consequentialist theories, the right is defined as that which maximizes the good, while deontological theories tend to downplay or ignore such relations.)

THE STUDENT:

That sounds promising.

THE ECONOMIST:

In practice, utilitarianism is a broad school of thought.[172]

THE CLASSICIST:

If you will, please allow me to press my point about the danger of bribery to the overall economy in addition to any moral concerns. I argued, right at the start of our discussions, that the main beneficiaries of bribery are likely to be those who abuse their power. I'm thinking of the monopolist, the rent-seeking civil servant, and even the gangster. Bribery involves acts of collusion in mutually advantageous transactions that are usually outside the law. When a culture of bribery sets the tone of a society, surely there are a vast range of costs that weigh on society as a whole, and many of these costs are likely to be invisible, or at least difficult to measure, because they reflect economic activity that is stunted or destroyed through bribery.[173] Market prices are

---

[172] The economist does not distinguish between act utilitarianism and rule utilitarianism. It is inconceivable that a professional economist would not be fully conversant with these matters: Perhaps he intends to keep the discussion non-technical. Act utilitarianism is based on the consequences of individual actions, while rule utilitarianism is founded on an action's conformity with a rule that in turn can be assessed on the basis of maximum utility.

[173] Compare Sowell (2015, 395): "Because scarce resources have alternative uses, the real costs [of bribery] are the foregone alternatives—delayed or aborted economic activity, the enterprises that are not started, the investments that are not made, the expansion of output and employment that does not take place in a thoroughly corrupt society, as well as the loss of skilled, educated and entrepreneurial people who leave the country".

surely distorted by bribes and other irregular transactions, and I suspect that the overall costs of bribery might be very extensive.[174]

THE ECONOMIST:

I think we need to be clear about the starting and ending points of my arguments. You might be right in saying that bribery can undermine a market as well as a country's more general social and political well-being. But my starting point is a market that is already ruined or stunted by factors such as over-regulation, political corruption, and artificial controls over supply or demand. Bribery thrives when markets and their supporting institutions are distorted or imperfect.[175] To give an example, look at independent India. After colonial rule ended, a system of corrupt governance became entrenched. Permits and licenses became required for most types of economic activity, and many civil servants abused the system to extort bribes.[176] If you're caught in such a "permit Raj" system, in which massive government interference and a corrupt bureaucracy cripples the markets, then

---

[174] Klitgaard (1988, 46) identifies the following as being among the costs of corruption: (1) wasted resources resulting from damage to economic efficiency, (2) skewed distribution of resources (with reallocation "to the rich"), (3) distorted incentives (with the skewing of the "energies of officials and citizens towards the socially unproductive"), and (4) damage to politics (with the breeding of "popular alienation and cynicism"). He also points out (24–25) that the costs of reducing corruption to zero may be unnecessarily costly and that a society may therefore have to accommodate itself to some level of ineradicable corruption.

[175] Compare Ezrow and Frantz (2013, 257) who suggest that widespread corruption may be a sign that institutions are not functioning properly and that the capacity of the state is declining.

[176] Sowell (2015, 272): "The vast array of government rules in India, micro-managing businesses, ensured that every businessman would break some law or the other every month." The liberalization of the modern Indian economy started only in the 1990s.

it makes sense to pay bribes to facilitate your activities. Bribery flourishes in such conditions, and we shouldn't condemn the individuals who respond rationally to the situation by making bribes.

THE PRIEST:

You've gone too far, and I can't agree with you.

THE ECONOMIST:

Oh?

THE PRIEST:

I remain concerned that your utilitarian considerations offer us a moral spectacle of the utmost bleakness. They seem to be based purely on functionalism and materialism. They are based on crass ideas of calculation and philistine economics, devoid of meaningful moral content.[177] Just because bribery may have a social function, in my view that is an insufficient reason for justifying it. After all, child marriage and slavery have also had social functions, and indeed continue to do so in some parts of the world, but it doesn't make them morally acceptable.[178] The ethically hollow victory of the successful briber might lubricate a small part of the economy but, with the logic of a monkey sawing through the branch it's sitting on, I suspect that the briber is contributing to a disastrous, overall ethical ruining of his society that goes far beyond the individual transaction.

---

[177] This is perhaps an echo of the criticisms of the "technological-Benthamite culture" by F.R. Leavis (1895–1978).

[178] Noonan (1984, 694) puts forward similar arguments.

THE ECONOMIST:

Your point is well taken. There has been much criticism of *homo economicus,*[179] that creature severed from morality, and some of it has been justified. But I can't really see a parallel between improving human well-being and prosperity in the manner I'm proposing and the reductive, ugly practices that you mention. Please remember that I'm talking about economic activity in legal systems that are not robust, impartial, or fair. When the law makes honesty costly, then the state is, effectively, promoting dishonesty, and it's unfair to haul the individuals trapped in such circumstances before a heavenly court of morals.[180]

THE STUDENT:

In any case, as far as I'm concerned, morality is made and remade by humans. It doesn't come from heaven.

THE ECONOMIST:

On that matter, I would tend to agree with you. However, please allow me to finish the discussion points I intended to raise regarding gifts and bribery. We're often told that the best way to reduce small-scale bribery is the full use of mechanisms like the justice system, an open press, and administrative accountability. And, of course, this is true to an extent. But I'm reminded of our earlier discussion of

---

[179] *Homo economicus* is "a rational, self-serving being whose actions and choices are based on logical decisions, not rash impulses" (Fisman and Miguel, 2008, 6). See also Fisman and Golden (2017, 5–12) for an analysis of contingent behavior that depends on others' actions, in the form of rational economic choices delinked from morality.

[180] Compare Ferguson (2012, 59): "The rule of law has many enemies. One of them is bad law."

religious scrupulosity,[181] which warned against an obsessive fear of rooting out all possible sins. Scrupulosity leads to psychological and emotional paralysis. Similarly, I would argue, excessive regulation of potential bribes may be counterproductive, especially in the weak and dysfunctional markets I've been describing. A moral crusade or witch hunt against minor bribes is likely to lead to more harm than good, at least in the short term.[182]

THE CLASSICIST:

You make a fair point. Obsessive attention on antibribery regulations may make matters worse, not only in badly governed societies where the rule of law is already weak, and where people therefore rely on small bribes as a survival mechanism, but also in the developed economies. The over-regulation of small bribes might lead to an unwarranted focus on moral purity to the detriment of the economy.[183] So I worry about the explosion in regulation relating to so-called anticorruption.[184]

---

[181] See n. 81.

[182] Velasquez (2012, 485) suggests that under some circumstances corruption can lower red tape and thereby increase efficiency, and that where corruption is "deeply entwined in a nation's political and cultural institutions, corruption has a stabilizing effect and so the [sudden] elimination of corruption could lead to instability and anarchy".

[183] Compare Ferguson (2012, 14): "[V]ery complex regulation has become the disease of which it purports to be the cure, distorting and corrupting both the political and economic process." Also Mayer (2013, 61): Excessive regulation results in "a system that confuses rules with standards, compliance with compassion, and obedience with integrity".

[184] This may be an allusion to the accelerated regulatory developments of the last decade of the twentieth century and the early twenty-first century (in which international organizations like the Organisation for Economic Co-operation and Development have been prominent). It may also allude to the 1990s Italian *mani pulite* ("clean hands") campaign of judicial investigation into corruption, and the exposition of the culture of the *tangentopoli* ("bribesville") (Ezrow and Frantz, 2013, 257).

THE ECONOMIST:

Exactly. We can't tout the success of an anticorruption drive just by counting the number of arrests or convictions or media headlines. We must look beyond those results to the costs of alternatives and, in particular, the time and expenditure wasted on trivial matters. I'm deeply concerned by the ever-increasing layers of regulation and control.[185] If, as you say, small-scale bribery can have corrosive effects on society, the same can be said for antibribery control systems, especially if they're too extensive and absolutist.[186] We must rein in the excesses of these crusading, anticorruption warriors.[187]

---

[185] Anechiarico and Jacobs (1996, 18–26) identify, for the United States, four overlapping yet distinct stages in the development of systems of anticorruption controls: (1) an "anti-patronage" era, focused on the establishment of an objective, public-serving civilized service (1870–1900), (2) a "progressive vision" that aimed to reform the political system (1900–1933), (3) a "scientific administration" vision founded on bureaucratic controls and management theory (1933–1970), and (4) a "panoptic" vision that aims at a comprehensive and intrusive system of regulation, surveillance, auditing, and oversight (1970 to the present day). The panoptic vision evokes Jeremy Bentham's "panopticon prison" and its extrapolation by Michel Foucault (1926–1984), in his *Surveiller et punir: Naissance de la prison* (1975), to a wider theory of a disciplinary and oppressive society that attempts to stamp out all kinds of "deviance". Anechiarico and Jacobs suggest that, under the "panoptic vision", the processes of surveillance and oversight run the risks of becoming ends in themselves rather than means to improvement. See also the analysis given by Åkerström (2014) of the negative impact of what he characterizes as the "bribery gaze" on everyday gift-giving and social courtesies, and Power (1999) on the proliferation of surveillance through auditing.

[186] Compare Anechiarico and Jacobs (1996, 183): An excessive anticorruption drive "reinforces bureaucracy as well as bureaucratic pathologies" and "contributes to the chronic problems of bureaucracy like decision-making delay, over-centralization, inadequate authority, goal displacement, defensive management, low morale, and inability to foster flexible solutions to problems".

[187] Sampson (2005) talks of "integrity warriors" in his analysis of the activities of Transparency International.

THE CLASSICIST:

And now are we going to hear the counter-narrative that we've been promised?[188]

THE ECONOMIST:

Yes, it's time. And then we'll try to summarize everything we've heard.

---

[188] "We've been promised": in Section Four.

Chapter Six
Inequities of Power

THE STUDENT:

Well, gentlemen, I've been sitting through our discussions, listening to a series of tired, old narratives that attempt to fix, once and for all, an ethical basis for understanding bribery. You've ransacked the Bible, and you've looted the texts of the Greek philosophers, and you've taken it for granted that there is a continuity between those ancient documents and our modern culture. And you've also proposed an economic consequentialist approach that, it is claimed, rests on rational choices of maximizing utility. Furthermore, you've based your arguments very much on patriarchal foundations that marginalize the feminine perspective. And I suspect the feminine perspective to be very different from what we've been hearing when it comes to bribery.[189] I shall present a very critical stance vis-à-vis all such grand narratives.

---

[189] Swamy et al. (2001) suggest that women tend to be less involved in bribery than men and are less likely to condone it. In addition, their research indicates that corruption tends to be lower in countries in which women hold greater positions of power (e.g. parliamentary seats or upper civil service posts). Noonan (1984, xvii–xviii, 25 and 141) draws attention to commonalities between (largely masculine) attitudes towards bribery and patriarchal sexual attitudes, including overlapping terminologies of "purity", "filth", and "betrayal".

THE CLASSICIST:

Interesting.

THE STUDENT:

To start with, when we speak about a social practice like bribery, we've entered into a discourse about power. It's clear to me that the relations between bribery and justice are necessarily uncertain. They're contingent on social conditions and the struggle for power between competing elites. In particular, a decision to define a gift as a bribe, and to punish it or to denounce it, is closely tied to who controls the levers of social and economic power.

THE PRIEST:

How, then, would you identify a bribe?

THE STUDENT:

A bribe, in my view, is essentially an abuse of power that causes harm and undermines social harmony and a sense of community.[190]

---

[190] Compare Dion (2014, 98–100) on bribery as an abuse of power. He describes corruption as a dehumanizing process that uses people as a means to an end and banishes true consensus from human relationships, thereby undermining attempts to establish a genuine sense of community. He writes: "Financial crimes are dehumanizing the world, insofar as they are reducing the intensity of mutual trust and understanding" (xxi). On the treatment of individuals as a means to an end rather than an end in themselves, compare Kant's second formulation of his categorical imperative: "Act so that you treat humanity, whether in your own person or that of another, always at the same time as an end, and never just as a means." (quoted in MacIntyre, 1998: xiii)

THE ECONOMIST:

I find nothing disagreeable in what you've said so far. It's clear that whoever wields the levers of power will be able to impose their views on the rest of society. They're bound to craft laws to suit their purposes.

THE STUDENT:

But there's more to it than that. Structural power relations determine pretty much all we see in the treatment of bribery today. Bribery is part of a complex web of social power relations. Laws can be established and flouted by those who can get away with it. Ethical standards can be institutionalized and propagated to subdue sections of society. And entrenched elites can bribe their way to personal enrichment as they establish social and legal mechanisms to protect their interests.

And it's not just a domestic issue: The international bribery narrative has Orientalist[191] overtones. We've already discussed the troubling side effects of the anticorruption drive in developing countries. I would add that this appears to me to be a symptom of a neo-imperialist movement to control, undermine, and ultimately exploit the so-called Third World.[192]

THE PRIEST:

There are undoubtedly grains of truth in what you're saying, but I think you're going too far.

---

[191] See n. 143.

[192] The collection of articles edited by Whyte (2015) explores the "myths" surrounding perceptions of the United Kingdom as a largely corruption-free, liberal democracy with a strong rule of law, in which acts like bribery are confined to the margins of public life, in contrast to perceptions of "Third World" corruption. In particular, the introduction (5–7) draws attention to a colonialist narrative of the West bringing order to "corrupt" and "primitive" parts of the world.

THE STUDENT:

Not at all. In the direct colonial era, the narrative was that the West brought science and modern governance to backward, tribal, and superstitious societies. The anticorruption narratives of the West today, and especially the discourses of the Western-controlled international organizations, are simply continuations of the old colonialist narratives. We're encouraged to believe that a dishonest, lazy, and decadent developing world needs to be disciplined and improved by a rational, scientific, and ethical West. At its roots, we see the same imperialistic desire to control vulnerable societies under the pretext of forcing a zealous reform program on them. There are immense asymmetries of power involved here, and these power differentials are easily exploited.

THE CLASSICIST:

You do have a point. Old prejudices die hard, and there is certainly an argument that can be made that exploitation of the Third World continues...

THE ECONOMIST:

(Interrupting) ...and it's certainly arrogant of the West to think that it can ethically cleanse the poorer parts of the world.

THE CLASSICIST:

But you seem almost to be saying that the poverty and corruption of the Third World are simply figments of our prejudiced imaginations and that such corruption is all socially constructed and therefore, so to speak, not really real. I've encountered many radicals who seem to deny reality.

THE STUDENT:

I don't deny reality. We're all here right now, sitting around this table. If I swing my leg and stub my toe on the table, then I'll hurt myself. So I know I'm really here. The table's really here, too. And my sore toe would confirm that reality, if I were foolish enough to stub it. Similarly, if I pass you an envelope stuffed with cash, then that would really be an envelope stuffed with cash. Physical reality is physical reality. But what I'm questioning is how we interpret that envelope stuffed with cash. For what purposes is it given? As a gift? A bribe? And whose interests would such interpretations serve?

If you believe the Bible is the word of God, or if you base your worldview on Platonic Forms or economic efficiency, you'll interpret the envelope full of cash according to your ideology. It's clear to me that we construct our individual interpretations of reality based on our worldviews, and these in turn are conditioned by social factors, especially in terms of structural and institutional power. A short time ago, I discussed modern Western appropriations of ancient Greek culture,[193] and similarly we must carefully review, with a critical eye, all claims to absolute truth.

THE PRIEST:

You make a good case, it seems to me, that we all carry individual and social prejudices. I can agree with you on that, but I wish to dig a little deeper into your arguments. Is your understanding of bribery largely reducible to power politics and social counter-narratives?

THE STUDENT:

That's a very abbreviated statement of my argument.

---

[193] In Section Four.

THE PRIEST:

Well, despite what you said about the pain of stubbing one's toe, I'm troubled by what appears to be your denial of absolute truth. You seem to be saying that any understanding of bribery is contingent on our prejudices, as well as on the social context and the narratives of those in power. To me, such arguments are little more than an attempt to avoid reality, and those who propagate such notions betray an attitude that they are somehow purer than the rest of us. As far as I'm concerned, such views are signs of moral emptiness. You're reducing moral judgment to mere personal preferences.

THE STUDENT:

Absolutely not. I believe I'm facing up to social reality.

THE CLASSICIST:

The arguments we've just heard assume that power relations are also relations of oppression and should therefore be overturned in the name of liberation. That is simply a form of ideology.

THE STUDENT:

Ideology? You're saying that I'm ideological? What I've been doing is unmasking the ideologies of much of what we've been discussing.

THE CLASSICIST:

I fear that, by trying not to be ideological, you risk falling into your own trap. Your denial of ideology is itself an ideological statement.

THE STUDENT:

Then how would you define the term "ideology"?

THE CLASSICIST:

I'd say that an ideology is an attempt to present as permanent truths concepts that are really no more than passing social fashions. A transient ideology has no light to shed on the enduring truths of the human condition.

THE PRIEST:

I agree. If we base our views on these critical and counter-narrative ideologies, we'll end up reading too much into things. After all, as Freud once said, sometimes a cigar is just a cigar.[194] If we overanalyze things and become excessively skeptical, we risk drowning in a sea of relativism and subjectivity. Excessive skepticism can be as damaging as excessive credulity. Ultimately, we risk being de-moralized, in the sense of being without moral standards. I'm sorry to be blunt, but in your worldview, everything is simply a grubby power struggle. Nothing is sacred!

THE STUDENT:

I expected such reactions. What I'm saying is radical, and it provokes intense displeasure from those with reactionary views. I'd also like to add another aspect to my argument: Concepts of justice are often distorted by language. The manipulation of language and the control over channels of communication are additional aspects of the way power relations make themselves felt. Attempts to articulate

---

[194] Apocryphal saying attributed to Sigmund Freud (1856–1939). See Kreeft (2018, 95).

a purportedly objective truth often mask the plurality of meanings that underpin all social practices.[195]

THE PRIEST:

I see. Then I'm confirmed in my suspicion of what appears to be your denial of absolute truth.

THE CLASSICIST:

But the point about language is an important one. The use of euphemisms can be a means of distancing oneself from an ugly truth. For example, describing a bribe as a gift may make it seem less immoral.[196]

THE STUDENT:

I respect the views I'm hearing around this table, but I don't share them. The problems are more fundamental than mere language games. You've discussed your worldview in terms of divine commands of universal validity, set out in ancient Eastern Mediterranean texts and developed by traditions in patriarchal institutions. My arguments run contrary to yours: I'm saying that concepts of justice and bribery are contingent

---

[195] See Candreva (2005, 25): For postmodernists like Jean-Francois Lyotard, justice is "merely a language-game; though it has rules establishing rules of behavior, these reflect agreements rather than truths and thus cannot have external justification". Thus, "justice is not a singular but rather a plural term, consisting of multiple 'justices', each with its own rules and practices".

[196] Bicchieri and Ganegoda (2017, 184) describe four psychological processes by which an individual can induce "ethical fading" (i.e. reducing the ethical significance of one's actions): (1) the use of euphemisms, (2) "slippery slope" notions of helplessness when faced by gradual increases in ethical deviations, (3) errors in perceptual causation, and (4) constraints induced by representation of the self. On broader considerations of forensic linguistics and bribery, see Shuy (2013).

on and influenced by power relations, official narratives and counter-narratives, and by negotiation and conflict. There is, to put it simply, no absolute truth on social practices like bribery.

THE CLASSICIST:

Are you really dismissing all we've been discussing up to this point? We've already made it clear that one doesn't need to have a religious commitment in order to identify the existence of objective truth. But you appear to be saying that a concept like bribery has absolutely no foundation in objectivity. So, it would appear, bribery has no inherent meaning: It is, allegedly, socially and culturally negotiated. Isn't this nihilism? A belief in nothing?

THE STUDENT:

I think that the term "nihilism", as you're using it, is simply another example of a power relations narrative. Those who are intellectually committed to a simple narrative of purported objective truth cannot handle a rejection of their abstract, universal principles and meta-narratives. They are lost when challenged over divine sanctions, objective truth, and Platonic Forms. A more accurate portrayal of social and moral concepts is based on dissent instead of consensus, plurality rather than singularity, and fluidity rather than stability.

THE CLASSICIST:

Objectivity isn't a sham. Timeless standards exist. There *is* an objective morality. Justice, the virtue most offended by bribery, really exists! The new ideological orthodoxy would have us believe that objectivity is a chimera, and there is no fixed reality of justice on which we can rely. But I'd argue that knowledge and high culture have an insuperable advantage over majority opinion and politicized ignorance.

THE ECONOMIST:

Well, my arguments were not founded on any allegedly timeless truths but rather on patterns of behavior in fluid settings like markets. I support the view that morality is man-made and variable, but I cannot go so far as to deny absolute truth.

THE CLASSICIST:

I hope you'll forgive me if I go back to Plato, as he addressed the issues of relativism and nihilism nearly two and a half thousand years ago. In terms of relativism, I cannot avoid thinking of Protagoras, a well-known sophist in ancient Greece. Socrates clashed with him,[197] in particular over his relativism. Protagoras was notorious for his saying that "Man is the measure of all things." Under his moral relativism, truth and value were determined by subjective opinion, which usually means the majority opinion. Protagoras suggested that morality was like an arbitrary linguistic sign: Just as languages vary between communities, for him so did morality, with no underlying truth, merely convention.

THE PRIEST:

And Socrates countered this relativism with arguments in favor of transcendent reality.

THE CLASSICIST:

Precisely. Modern-day Protagoreans are the moral relativists of our times. For them, morality is a matter of opinion or a

---

[197] Plato, *Protagoras*.

social construct that reflects current economic and social power structures. In their eyes, opinions matter more than facts. And in *Gorgias*, Plato gives us a portrayal of Callicles, a rather unsavory character who considers ethical standards to be simply part of power politics and a means of bending the community to one's will. Callicles is convinced that people will indulge in unjust actions if they believe they can get away with it.[198] So, for the purposes of our discussion, Callicles would consider a bribe simply to be a means of exercising power, with no inherent moral significance. For Socrates, in contrast, it's better to suffer injustice than to do injustice, and bribery is wrong. Socrates understood the moral worth of justice. We're talking of a fundamental conflict of world visions. In short, Protagorean relativists and Calliclean nihilists are the philosophical ancestors of today's critical theorists and deniers of reality.[199]

THE STUDENT:

I suppose that's why Plato put into Socrates's mouth his arguments in favor of the inherent harmony of the cosmos, based on the fanciful reality of the Forms.

THE CLASSICIST:

Plato did so, in my view, in a manner that established an unanswerable case for the existence of objective truth in

---

[198] The speaker might also have mentioned the comments of Thrasymachus in *Republic* 338c: "I say that justice is nothing other than the advantage of the stronger", which implies that justice is not a universal value but rather a concept related to the expedient actions of socially dominant individuals or groups.

[199] Plato, *Gorgias* 504d–e: Socrates says to Callicles that, in terms of justice, a "good orator", in "all of his actions, and any gift he makes...will always give his attention to how justice may come to exist in the souls of his fellow citizens and injustice be gotten rid of...and how the rest of excellence may come into being there and badness may depart".

moral matters. In *Gorgias*, Plato portrayed the difficulty of communication at an existential level in a corrupt and decadent society. There are clear parallels with our age. I maintain that Protagoras and Callicles are still around, and they're in charge not only of our universities but also of many, or most, of our political systems.

THE STUDENT:

I find your comments exaggerated. I think they support my position that the defenders of orthodox dogmas tend to become somewhat aggressive when their orthodoxies are challenged.

THE CLASSICIST:

It's not my intention to be anything other than fair and polite.

THE STUDENT:

Then let me challenge some of the central features of your assertions. How can you justify the simplistic theory of Platonic Forms in the modern era? There's no scientific or logical basis for such a theory. Isn't it little more than a fairy tale?

THE CLASSICIST:

Definitely not. The Forms are a serious and convincing attempt to understand the nature of reality, and not just in terms of physical objects. They explain the existence of truth in matters like justice and beauty.[200]

---

[200] Plato's *Seventh Letter* (342–345) has an excellent summary of the Platonic Forms (although the authenticity of the letter is disputed).

THE STUDENT:

We're talking about metaphysical speculation. It's hardly convincing in our modern, or postmodern, world.

THE CLASSICIST:

On that we'll have to agree to disagree. Plato made a helpful distinction, now lost in our vocabulary, between the philosopher as the lover of wisdom and the philodoxer, the lover of opinion.[201] The philodoxer is the opponent of the philosopher because he or she is a nihilist, devoid of ethics, and interested only in the manipulations of power politics.

THE STUDENT:

So Plato was the vehicle of eternal truths, and the rest of us are simply opinion peddlers, the victims of circumstance and misunderstanding?

THE CLASSICIST:

Look, Plato never claimed that his Forms were easy to apprehend. In one of Plato's dialogues,[202] Socrates described himself as a philosophical midwife, in the sense that he wasn't imparting a doctrine of his own but instead assisting others to generate their own philosophical understandings. Socrates or Plato may have been ironic in saying this, as Socrates's use of irony is well known. Nonetheless, the relentless search for definitions[203] seems to have contributed to the theory of Forms, even though Socrates admitted that he wasn't sure

---

[201] See the comments of Voegelin (2000, 125–135) on "the sophistic doxa of justice".

[202] *Theaetetus* 149a–150d.

[203] See n. 23.

about the precise way in which the Forms relate to us and the physical world.[204]

THE STUDENT:

You've accused me of escaping from reality, as you understand it, but I maintain that your Platonic Forms are simply a metaphysical fairy tale.

THE ECONOMIST:

Fair enough. I think we need to move our discussions along now to avoid getting bogged down in circular and repetitive arguments.

THE CLASSICIST:

Please indulge us for a few moments more because this part of the discussion touches on the deepest concepts of reality. How can we assess the ethical values surrounding bribery if we can't even agree on whether bribery is real?

THE PRIEST:

Yes, I think this discussion is worth pursuing a little more.

THE CLASSICIST:

Then permit me to say that Plato's Theory of Forms is not an escape from the structure of reality but an invitation to understand and participate in it. The Forms are the grounding of the world. The Forms of justice and other matters are perfect paradigms and universal realities. They're intangible, yet they're even more real than the physical things we can

---

[204] *Phaedo* 101d.

see and touch. Beyond the world available to our senses is a deeper reality that cannot be observed but only grasped by the mind. Therefore, Plato would say that the things we can see and touch are only half real: They belong to a middle realm between reality and unreality.

Numbers are clearly universal, abstract entities like the Forms; the number three is the same everywhere and doesn't depend on opinion or culture. Three is three, whether here right now or in the Mughal Empire or in prehistoric Australia. Similarly, justice is justice everywhere, at all times. And bribery is bribery everywhere, at all times. Of course, this doesn't imply that we don't need to apply judgment and interpretation to understand what we encounter. Nonetheless, hidden, eternal unities underpin the transient multiplicities we see.

So the Forms can't be seen by the body's physical eye. They can only be seen by the mind's eye. They are perfect and eternal, but the extent to which we, individually or collectively, participate in a form like justice may be only partial. For Plato, our life on earth can be likened to a subterranean existence from which we perceive only occasional glimpses of the eternal sunlight of the forms.

THE STUDENT:

You've expressed your point of view well, but I remain unconvinced. You claim that actions have an intrinsic value, but I place more importance on how we interpret them and how they interact with social power hierarchies.

THE CLASSICIST:

It's clear that Plato considered the Forms to be unchanging realities. Therefore, he considered the virtues to be unchanging realities. The virtues are therefore real and beyond time and space. They differ from the transitory nature of opinions.

The modern aversion to metaphysics and our culture of relativism have made the Platonic Theory of Forms seem untenable to many. Many would have us believe that the quest for truth is a Socratic or Platonic fallacy. The rational quest for certainty in human affairs is not popular today.

THE STUDENT:

Or perhaps the search for truth has taken new, and more realistic, directions. Just because there are traditions claiming access to permanent truths, it doesn't mean that we all have to step into line behind them. Our understanding of ideas and concepts often has roots in biological, social, and political conditions that are deeper than documented traditions.

THE CLASSICIST:

All I would add is that Plato didn't leave us with a fixed dogma of the Forms. On the contrary, he left us with much ambiguity. One difficulty with the Forms is the differences in the way they are presented between Plato's dialogues. Some readers think that Plato had a single teaching on the Forms and that the dialogues simply explore different aspects of this teaching; others believe that Plato developed his views over his life and that this accounts for the differences in the way the Forms are presented in different dialogues. To me, any ambiguities in the presentation of the Forms are secondary to the main argument of their existence. Plato leaves to the readers of his dialogues the task of thinking about the Forms. Plato's writings don't provide a closed system of ideological truth. They remain a challenge to us. They encourage us to assess whether reality exists and whether we can use our reason to understand it. This is separate from any religious belief, though it can be reconciled with religion, as we've seen.[205] And the Forms aren't a metaphysical fairy tale: They're the establishment of a secure order of reality here on earth.[206]

THE PRIEST:

I find myself in agreement with much, or most, of what you say. But didn't Aristotle largely reject the Theory of Forms?

THE CLASSICIST:

No, I don't think so. This is a huge topic in itself, but I'd say that Aristotle offered a different, more "grounded" approach to reality. He certainly questioned the Platonic Forms but didn't necessarily reject them.[207] He tried to bring them more obviously down to earth, so to speak.

THE ECONOMIST:

Alright. Thank you for these insights. Now I propose that we move on to...

---

[205] See Section Four. On the secular nature of the Forms, compare Candreva (2005, 33): "The Platonic pilot who gazes heavenward is not consulting the gods but instead is employing a very practical form of knowledge."

[206] Compare the warnings of Kosman (2007, 136–137) against temptations to interpret Plato as overly metaphysical: "We misread Plato disastrously when we read him in light of a Gnostic otherworldliness that pictures the forms as resident in a place far, far away from ours, rather than as the principles of the intelligibility of this...world. It is as disastrous a misreading to portray the forms as ontological tyrants designed to stamp out diversity, difference, and otherness."

[207] See Dillon (2003, passim).

THE CLASSICIST:

One final thing, please. For Plato, not all the Forms were equal. The most important Form was the Good, as we see in the *Republic*, and the other Forms are subordinate to it. And the next two most important Forms are probably Beauty, in the *Symposium*, and Justice, in the *Republic*. And in our discussion today we have focused on how bribery damages justice.

THE ECONOMIST:

Alright. I know this issue has raised some passionate viewpoints, and I think it will be hard to reconcile the views we've heard about the nature of reality. In any case, I wish now to proceed to try to wrap up what our discussions have revealed.

THE PRIEST:

Not an easy task.

THE CLASSICIST:

Indeed.

Chapter Seven
Closing Discussions

THE ECONOMIST:

We've just heard a fairly strong disagreement over the nature of reality in terms of social phenomena. However, I think that, overall, we might be able to come away with some positive overall conclusions from our discussions. There appears to be nothing new under the sun[208] when it comes to bribery. Indeed, bribery has a long and twisted history, and it seems to be an inescapable part of social and economic life— perhaps like prostitution. I see no need to amend our pithy definition of bribery as "minor, influence-peddling gifts".[209] We deliberately excluded grand corruption from our discussions, and our definition allowed us to focus on that fuzzy zone between gifts and bribes.

So, to come to the point, can bribery ever be virtuous? Is there such a thing as a "good bribe"? Firstly, we heard about duty-based ethical approaches to this question,[210] which suggested to us that bribery is inherently wrong because it tends to violate justice. The Bible and Plato left us with this legacy. Although I don't personally adhere to either biblical or Platonic concepts, I was pleasantly surprised to learn of the flexibility and scope for judgment embedded in the

---

[208] An allusion to *Ecclesiastes* 1:9.
[209] See n. 22.
[210] In Sections Two to Four.

biblical interpretations, especially in differentiating between a legitimate gift and a justice-denying bribe. It's rarely a neat, black-and-white matter. Judgment is needed to address the thorny issue of when a gift becomes a bribe.

Aristotle also reminded us that consistently ethical dispositions and ways of life are of crucial importance, and I added to our discussions my views on the economic consequences of gifts and bribes,[211] with a view to maximizing their utility, or benefits. I argued that it may be legitimate to pay a bribe in an environment that is itself corrupted. Patronage seems to be ineradicable, and bribery thrives on patronage: In such an environment, a bribe might be a self-defense mechanism or even a survival tactic. It may be a justifiable way of making economic transactions happen. In addition, there are occasions when a bribe smooths the way to a undeniably positive outcome: We mentioned the bribes paid by Oskar Schindler[212] to save lives during the Second World War. And we've just heard[213] arguments on the importance of taking into account the social and power relations that underpin bribery. One person's bribery may be another person's gift.

THE STUDENT:

Or one society's bribery may be another society's gift.

THE ECONOMIST:

Precisely. So I think we can say that bribery might be considered virtuous on occasions, especially when its consequences are positive or when it is forced on us, so to speak, by circumstances. But we should always bear in mind the social power structures in our interpretations.

---

[211] In Section Five.
[212] See n. 145.
[213] In Section Six.

THE PRIEST:

You've given a balanced overview of our discussions. But I still perceive plenty of irreconcilable aspects of what we've been saying. First of all, the differentiation between a gift and bribe is crucial, but it may be very difficult to draw the line in practice.

THE ECONOMIST:

I fully agree. That's why judgment plays such a crucial role.

THE STUDENT:

Indeed. I cannot envision how one could differentiate between a gift and a bribe without weighing the consequences for the power relations involved.

THE PRIEST:

I'd go further than considering only the consequences of a gift. Consequences matter, of course, but there's also the important matter of the nature and intentions of a gift. If we offer a gift in good faith, without the expectation of reciprocity, then it is indeed a gift and not a bribe.

THE CLASSICIST:

You've touched on a thorny issue. Don't all gifts, to some extent and at some level, have an inherent expectation of exchange and reciprocity?[214]

---

[214] The notion that a gift contains some inherent reciprocity was argued by Mauss (1925). The use of gift-giving to build long-term business and trading relationships is well known and implies reciprocal benefits arising from the gifts in such circumstances. However, the view of reciprocity in gift-giving has been challenged by, among others, Cheal (1988), Godbout

THE PRIEST:

Absolutely not. A gift can be given in the Christian sense of charity, or love, as an act of total selflessness. A gift, unlike a bribe, has no *quid pro quo*.

THE CLASSICIST:

Your point is well taken. Though let's not forget entirely that the intentions and social positions of those taking part in such transactions tend to be of overriding importance.

THE ECONOMIST:

The intentions and social positions? Yes, absolutely. But the consequences, too. I insist that the consequences of gift-giving cannot be overlooked.

THE CLASSICIST:

Fair enough.

THE PRIEST:

And when a gift that is undeniably a bribe is made, it is inherently wrong, it seems to me. I can accept the arguments of expediency in a corrupt environment, but this doesn't change the fact that the act of bribery is wrong in itself. I'd give the analogy of killing: It might be legitimate for a person to kill in self-defense or when acting as a soldier in a just war, but this doesn't make killing people a virtuous pastime. Similarly, a

---

and Caillé (2000), and Goffman (1967), who have argued that gift-giving is not necessarily exchange oriented but instead can be seen as a ritualistic social practice without expectation of reciprocity. For example, Godbout and Caillé suggest that "making the rule of reciprocity explicit kills the gift" (189).

bribe may sometimes be a positive act, yet that hardly makes bribery virtuous in principle.

THE CLASSICIST:

That's nicely put.

THE PRIEST:

Bribery is wrong in so many ways. It offends our sense of justice and destroys social trust.[215] It also rewards the powerful, and in this I agree with what's been said about the importance of taking social power into account in our judgments. There may be borderline cases, but by and large I think the difference between gifts and bribes is usually quite clear.[216]

THE STUDENT:

From my perspective, I think that bribery can be very damaging to both individuals and societies. I do think that notions of honesty, fair dealing, and respect for human dignity are remarkably similar in cultures in all regions of the world, which is not to say that there are many dissimilarities. I'm just not prepared to make the kinds of metaphysical commitments I've heard around this table today.

---

[215] Noonan (1984, 702–704) suggests four reasons for bribery being wrong: It is shameful; it is a sell-out to the rich ("deeper pockets will prevail"); it is a betrayal of trust; and it violates the divine paradigm of *imitatio dei*. See also n. 32.

[216] Compare Dion (2014, 103): There are "no gray areas between gifts and bribes. Unlike bribes, gifts are offered to maintain friendly relationships and have nothing to do with preferential treatment. Gift-giving practices are expressing neither an abuse of power, nor...dishonest behavior and intent. If some gifts are given in such state of mind...then they are indeed bribes".

THE ECONOMIST:

In that respect, I share your views to a large degree. And yet, I find that I have to reject as unacceptable a thoroughgoing relativism of all moral standards. However, I can live with a more modest relativism of ethical judgments, especially from a multicultural perspective. Also, over time, attitudes may change.[217]

THE CLASSICIST:

I'm going to make a statement now that may surprise you. I do see a way of reconciling what we've been saying. I don't claim that all the rough edges can be smoothed out, but we can harmonize our views to a large extent.

THE PRIEST:

How?

THE CLASSICIST:

I'm talking about ethical pluralism. We don't necessarily have to choose between duty-based ethics, virtue ethics, conse-quentialist ethics, specially constructed ethics, or economic rationality. Why can't we synthesize all this into an eclectic viewpoint? And maybe there are additional perspectives we haven't considered today.[218]

THE STUDENT:

That would seem an ambitious project.

---

[217] Compare Noonan (1984, xi): "[T]he concept of a bribe contracts or expands with conventions, laws, practices".

[218] For example, not covered in these discussions are the perspectives of cognitive neuroscience (Nichols and Robertson, 2017).

THE CLASSICIST:

But not an impossible one. We can accept the view that the intentions behind a gift matter. And its consequences. And we can also accept that power relations and economic calculation also have their part to play. And duty-based ethical perspectives can be accommodated alongside this. So we may have a plurality of perspectives. I think we need to try to bring to bear on the questions a large dose of common sense and perhaps also a maturity of emotional intelligence, and perhaps even a reliance on our intuitions.[219]

THE ECONOMIST:

What you're saying is not uninteresting.

THE PRIEST:

Yes, indeed. Perhaps we need to think along these lines. We may also consult the great works of art to inform us. Let's take, for example, the case of Wagner's *Ring*.[220] In it we see personifications of the eternal human condition. The overriding theme of this work of art is the never-ending battle between good and evil, in the form of love versus power. Wotan, with his spear carved with treaties, stands for power and narrow legalism. He's thoroughly corrupt, just like his subterranean mirror image Alberich. Everything revolves around power and wealth, and he fights to control the power of the ring that conveys mastery of the world. He tries to

---

[219] In the reference to common sense and intuition, the classicist may have in mind the arguments put forward by Ross (1930) for a "ground-level", pluralistic ethical viewpoint, in contrast to the "loftier" viewpoints of virtue ethics, deontological ethics, and utilitarianism.

[220] *Der Ring des Nibelungen*, the music drama tetralogy of Richard Wagner (1813–1883), composed between 1848 and 1874. The Wagner-loving priest's comments might, perhaps, bring to mind the music criticism of Father Owen Lee (for example, Lee, 1999).

manipulate those around him as though they were pieces on a chess board. But the theme of unconditional love bubbles under the surface, and it eventually triumphs through Brünnhilde, who sacrifices herself for love and destroys the corrupt world of the pagan gods. The *Ring* tells us that love defeats power.

THE STUDENT:

And the relevance of all this to bribery?

THE PRIEST:

Isn't it obvious? Love defeats power. That's the truth. In terms of bribery, the generosity of unconditional gift-giving is the crystallization of charity and love: This overcomes the evil of bribery. The heart defeats the wallet. A gift given with love and generosity has no intention of entrapment nor of subordinating the recipient to one's desires or needs. A gift given with love tramples on power politics and avoids the selfishness of the bribe.[221] This, perhaps, is where a consideration of intuition might lead us.

THE CLASSICIST:

I don't dislike what you're saying. However, I fear that you may be opening up another contentious area of discussion with your references to Wagner! This isn't to deny the validity of your comments, but surely, for today, we've adequately

---

[221]Compare Noonan (1984, 697): "A bribe expresses self-interest; a gift conveys love. A bribe subordinates the recipient to the donor; a gift identifies the donor with the recipient. A gift brings no shame; a bribe must be secret. A gift may be disclosed; a bribe must be concealed. The size of a gift is irrelevant; the size of a bribe, decisive. A gift does not oblige; a bribe coerces. A gift belongs to the donee; a bribe belongs to those to whom the bribe is accountable."

discussed in great detail a tricky subject. Maybe we should meet again to consider the lessons to be learned from great art in our understanding of bribery. Perhaps art will reach into our hearts and touch our deepest intuitions, where words fail to reach. It might well be that words cannot fully articulate the nature of the problem we've been reviewing.

THE ECONOMIST:

Be that as it may, I agree that we've had a valuable day's conversations. We might reconvene to try to reconcile our views or to seek artistic inspiration. But, for now, I think we deserve some wine and an enjoyable dinner.

THE CLASSICIST:

And I forbid any further mention today of the words "gift" and "bribe"!

THE ECONOMIST:

I'm sure we all heartily agree.

References

Adeney, Bernard T. *Strange Virtues: Ethics in a Multicultural World.* Downers Grove, IL: InterVarsity Press, 1995.

Åkerström, Malin. *Suspicious Gifts: Bribery, Morality, and Professional Ethics.* New Brunswick, NJ: Transaction Publishers, 2014.

Anechiarico, Frank and James B. Jacobs. *The Pursuit of Absolute Integrity: How Corruption Control Makes Government Ineffective.* Chicago: University of Chicago Press, 1996.

Ariely, Dan. *Predictably Irrational: The Hidden Forces That Shape Our Decisions.* New York: HarperCollins, 2008.

Bernal, Martin. *Black Athena: The Afroasiatic Roots of Classical Civilization* (3 vols.). New Brunswick, NJ: Rutgers University Press, 1987.

Bicchieri, Cristina and Deshani Ganegoda. "Determinants of Corruption: A Sociopsychological Analysis." In *Thinking about Bribery*, edited by Philip M. Nichols and Diana C. Robertson. Cambridge: Cambridge University Press, 2017.

Brickhouse, Thomas C. and Nicholas D. Smith. *The Trial and Execution of Socrates: Sources and Controversies.* New York: Oxford University Press, 2002.

Brioschi, Carlo Alberto. *Corruption: A Short History.* Washington, DC: Brookings Institution Press, 2017.

Candreva, Debra. *The Enemies of Perfection: Oakeshott, Plato, and the Critique of Rationalism.* Lanham, MD: Lexington Books, 2005.

Cheal, David. *The Gift Economy.* London: Routledge, 1988.

Cohen, Abraham. *Everyman's Talmud: The Major Teachings of the Rabbinic Sages*. London: J.M. Dent, 1932.

Colombatto, Enrico. "Why is Corruption Tolerated?" *The Review of Austrian Economics* 16, no. 4 (2003): 363–379.

Croall, Hazel. *Understanding White Collar Crime*. Buckingham: Open University Press, 2001.

Desbois, Father Patrick. *In Broad Daylight: The Secret Procedures behind the Holocaust by Bullets*. New York: Arcade Publishing, 2018.

Dillon, John. *The Heirs of Plato: A Study of the Old Academy, 347–274 B.C.* New York: Oxford University Press, 2003.

Dion, Michel. *Financial Crimes and Existential Philosophy*. New York: Springer, 2014.

Ehrman, Bart D. *Lost Christianities: The Battles for Scripture and the Faiths We Never Knew*. New York: Oxford University Press, 2003.

Ezrow, Natasha M. and Erica Frantz. *Failed States and Institutional Decay: Understanding Instability and Poverty in the Developing World*. London: Bloomsbury, 2013.

Ferguson, Niall. *Civilization: The West and the Rest*. London: Allen Lane, 2011.

Ferguson, Niall. *The Great Degeneration: How Institutions Decay and Economies Decline*. London: Allen Lane, 2012.

Fisman, Raymond and Edward Miguel. *Economic Gangsters: Corruption, Violence, and the Poverty of Nations*. Princeton: Princeton University Press, 2008.

Fisman, Raymond and Miriam A. Golden. *Corruption: What Everyone Needs to Know*. New York: Oxford University Press, 2017.

Foucault, Michel. *Surveiller et Punir: Naissance de la Prison*. Paris: Gallimard, 1975.

Fukuyama, Francis. *Origins of Political Order: From Prehuman Times to the French Revolution*. New York: Farrar Straus Giroux, 2011.

Gathercole, Simon. *The Gospel of Judas: Rewriting Early Christianity*. New York: Oxford University Press, 2007.

Godbout, Jacques and Alain C. Caillé. *The World of the Gift.* Montreal: McGill-Queen's University Press, 2000.

Goffman, Ervine. *Interaction Ritual: Essays on Face-to-Face Behavior.* New York: Aldine Publishing, 1967.

Gmirkin, Russell E. *Plato and the Creation of the Hebrew Bible.* Abingdon: Routledge, 2017.

Hanink, Johanna. *The Classical Debt: Greek Antiquity in an Era of Austerity.* Cambridge, MA: Belknap Press, 2017.

James, George. *Stolen Legacy: Greek Philosophy is Stolen Egyptian Philosophy.* New York: Julian Richardson, 1954.

Johnsen, Bruce D. "The Ethics of 'Commercial Bribery': Integrative Social Contract Theory Meets Transaction Cost Economics." *Journal of Business Ethics* 88 (2009): 791–803.

Kasser, Rodolphe, Marvin Meyer and Gregor Wurst. *The Gospel of Judas: Critical Edition.* Washington, DC: National Geographic Society, 2006.

Khalil, Fahad, Jacques Lawarrée and Sungho Yun. "Bribery versus Extortion: Allowing the Lesser of Two Evils." *RAND Journal of Economics* 41, no. 1 (2010): 179–198.

Klitgaard, Robert. *Controlling Corruption.* Berkeley: University of California Press, 1988.

Kosman, Aryeh. "Justice and Virtue: Inquiry into Proper Difference." In *The Cambridge Companion to Plato's Republic*, edited by G.R.F Ferrari, 116–137. Cambridge: Cambridge University Press, 2007.

Kreeft, Peter. *The Platonic Tradition.* South Bend, IN: St. Augustine's Press, 2018.

Lee, M. Owen. *Wagner: The Terrible Man and his Truthful Art.* Toronto: University of Toronto Press, 1999.

Leff, Nathaniel. "Economic Development Through Bureaucratic Corruption." *American Behavioral Scientist* 8, no. 3 (1964): 8–14.

MacIntyre, Alasdair. *A Short History of Ethics* (2nd ed.). London: Routledge, 1998.

Mauss, Marcel. "Essai sur le Don: Forme et Raison de l'Echange dans les Sociétés Archaïques." *L'Année Sociologique* (1925).

Mayer, Colin. *Firm Commitment: Why the corporation is failing us and how to restore trust in it.* Oxford: Oxford University Press, 2013.

Meyer, Marvin. *Judas: The Definitive Collection of Gospels and Legends about the Infamous Disciple of Jesus.* New York: HarperOne, 2007.

Nichols, Philip M. "The Good Bribe." *UC Davis Law Review* 49, no. 2 (2015): 647–683.

Nichols, Philip M. and Diana C. Robertson. *Thinking About Bribery: Neuroscience, Moral Cognition and the Psychology of Bribery.* Cambridge: Cambridge University Press, 2017.

Nikulin, Dmitri, ed. *The Other Plato: The Tübingen Interpretation of Plato's Inner-Academic Teachings.* New York: State University of New York, 2012.

Noonan, John T. *Bribes.* Berkeley: University of California Press, 1984.

North, Douglas, John Wallis and Barry Weingast. *Violence and Social Orders: A Conceptual Framework for Interpreting Recorded Human History.* Cambridge: Cambridge University Press, 2009.

Popper, Karl. *The Open Society and Its Enemies, Vol. I: The Spell of Plato.* London: Routledge, 1945.

Power, Michael. *The Audit Society: Rituals of Verification.* Oxford: Oxford University Press, 1999.

Rawls, John. *A Theory of Justice.* Cambridge, MA: Harvard University Press, 1971.

Reale, Giovanni. *Autotestimonianze e Rimandi dei Dialoghi di Platone alle "Dottrine Non Scritte."* Milan: Bompiani, 2008.

Rose-Ackerman, Susan. *Corruption and Government: Causes, Consequences, and Reform.* Cambridge: Cambridge University Press, 1999.

Ross, W.D. *The Right and the Good.* Oxford: Oxford University Press, 1930.

Sacks, Jonathan. *Exodus: The Book of Redemption.* London: Maggid, 2010.

Said, Edward. *Orientalism.* New York: Pantheon, 1978.

Sampson, Steven. "Integrity Warriors: Global Morality and the Anti-corruption Movement in the Balkans," In *Corruption: Anthropological Perspectives,* edited by Dieter Haller and Cris Shore. London: Pluto Press, 2005.

Samuel, Andrew. "Cognitive Dissonance, Ethical Behavior, and Bribery." In *Thinking about Bribery,* edited by Philip M. Nichols and Diana C. Robertson, 85–102. Cambridge: Cambridge University Press, 2017.

Sanyal, Rajib and Subarna Samanta. "Relationship between Bribery and Economic Growth: An Empirical Analysis." *Indian Journal of Economics & Business* 9, no. 1 (2010): 133–145.

Sarna, Nahum M. *The JPS Torah Commentary: Exodus.* Philadelphia: Jewish Publication Society, 1991.

Scruton, Roger. *Dictionary of Political Thought* (3rd ed.). Basingstoke: Palgrave Macmillan, 2007.

Senior, Ian. *Corruption—The World's Big C: Cases, Causes, Consequences, Cures.* London: Institute of Economic Affairs, 2006.

Shuy, Roger W. *The Language of Bribery Cases.* New York and Oxford: Oxford University Press, 2013.

Søreide, Tina. *Drivers of Corruption: A Brief Review.* Washington, DC: World Bank Group, 2014.

Sowell, Thomas. *Basic Economics: A Common Sense Guide to the Economy* (5th ed.). New York: Basic Books, 2015.

Swamy, Anand, Stephen Knack, Young Lee, and Omar Azfar. "Gender and Corruption." *Journal of Development Economics* 64, no. 1 (2001): 25–55.

Szlezák, Thomas A. *Reading Plato.* London: Routledge, 1999.

Tarán, Leonardo. *Speusippus of Athens.* Leiden: E.J. Brill, 1981.

Theobald, Robin. "So What is Really the Problem about Corruption?" *Third World Quarterly* 20, no. 3 (1999): 491–502.

Tullock, Gordon. *Selected Works of Gordon Tullock, Vol. 5: The Rent-Seeking Society,* edited by Charles K. Rowley. Indianapolis: Liberty Fund Inc., 2005.

Velasquez, Manuel. "Corruption and Bribery." In *Oxford Handbook of Business Ethics*, edited by George G. Brenkert and Tom L. Beauchamp, 471–500. New York and Oxford: Oxford University Press, 2012.

Voegelin, Eric. *Order and History, Vol. III: Plato and Aristotle.* In *The Collected Works of Eric Voegelin, Vol. 16.* Columbia: University of Missouri Press, 2000, originally published in 1957.

Warnock, Mary. *An Intelligent Person's Guide to Ethics.* London: Duckworth Books, 1998.

Warren, Robert Penn. *All the King's Men.* New York: Harcourt, 1946.

Whyte, David, ed. *How Corrupt is Britain?* London: Pluto Press, 2015.

CPSIA information can be obtained
at www.ICGtesting.com
Printed in the USA
FSHW011005030720
71531FS

9 781627 343008